THE WALL

BETWEEN
WOMEN

BETH
BRYKMAN

THE WALL

BETWEEN
WOMEN

THE CONFLICT BETWEEN
STAY-AT-HOME AND EMPLOYED MOTHERS

59 John Glenn Drive
Amherst, New York 14228-2197

Published 2006 by Prometheus Books

Inquiries should be addressed to
Prometheus Books
59 John Glenn Drive
Amherst, New York 14228–2197
VOICE: 716–691–0133, ext. 207
FAX: 716–564–2711
WWW.PROMETHEUSBOOKS.COM

10 09 08 07 06   5 4 3 2 1

Library of Congress Cataloging-in-Publication Data

Brykman, Beth.
    The wall between women : the conflict between stay-at-home and employed
mothers / by Beth Brykman.
        p. cm.
    Includes bibliographical references and index.
    ISBN 1–59102–394–7 (pbk. : alk. paper)
    1. Working mothers. 2. Stay-at-home mothers. 3. Mothers—Conduct of life.
4. Mothers—Attitudes. 5. Working mothers—Public opinion. 6. Stay-at-home
mothers—Public opinion. I. Title.

HQ759.48.B78 2006
331.4′4—dc22

                                                           2005035133

Printed in the United States of America on acid-free paper

CONTENTS

CONTENTS

CONTENTS

About a year ago, I was at a Newcomers' wine-tasting party when Ronnie, a newly found friend of mine, came up to me and started talking about how the mothers in her neighborhood were shunning her. She was a director of procurement at a Fortune 500 company, working long hours in a powerful position, while most of the other moms in her neighborhood stayed at home, with their careers in the past or on the back burner.

Ronnie claimed, "The biggest challenge is talking with these mothers. As a full-time career mom, I am stuck in the middle. I feel that I have more in common with the men at the neighborhood picnics than the women, yet I wanted to converse with the other mothers and be part of the neighborhood. When I ask them, 'How do you spend your day?' the reply is, 'You sound just like my husband,' very defensive. I really want to know what she does all day, as I am thinking of staying home myself and have no idea what this change in lifestyle means for me."

As a full-time career mom in a neighborhood filled with at-home mothers, Ronnie felt like a loner, not fitting in on her home turf. I was stunned. Was Ronnie alone, or do other career moms feel it, too? It led me to wonder whether this was just an employed mother's perspective—or whether this Wall was felt by stay-at-home mothers as well?

With my background, training, and business experience in marketing, I decided to attack this question as a market research project. Having been a full-time employed mom, a part-time working mother, as well as a stay-at-home mom myself, I realized that our experiences can vastly change our responses to each other. With that in mind, I began interviewing all kinds of mothers—ones with various-aged children (babies to seniors in high school), ones who were factory workers, doctors, secretaries, copy writers, bankers, house cleaners, advertising executives, tour guides, and lawyers.

INTRODUCTION

I set up the project using the same qualitative research techniques that Fortune 100 corporations use to develop multimillion-dollar products. I formally interviewed over one hundred mothers individually, using a preset, open-ended questionnaire and taking notes throughout the conversations. To avoid a regional bias on the overall topic, I interviewed approximately a quarter of the mothers from the Northeast, a quarter from the Southeast, a quarter from the middle section of the country, and the final quarter from the Western states. (Please see the appendix for further research details.) The book is written in a conversational style for ease and pleasure of reading. In order for each woman to remain anonymous, the names in this book are fictitious, but the vocations, stories, and feelings are very real.

After eight months of conducting the structured interviews, I would mention my writing to new people whom I met. Once female acquaintances heard about the topic, they could not stop discussing it with me whether I was rafting on the Colorado River, walking the dog, or attending my husband's corporate Christmas party. Women wanted to talk about this. Informally, I gathered even more stories and information regarding mothers' thoughts, confirming what I had already learned.

I initiated conversations with mothers by saying, "I believe that there is a Wall between full-time working mothers and stay-at-home mothers. What is your reaction to that?" The responses aided me in defining the cultural struggle between dissimilar mothers and describing the dynamics of the Wall.

WHY A WALL EXISTS

To understand why this Wall is built, we have to understand that our society in the United States has come to a crossroad. Women today can *choose* to have a successful career, to be the primary caretaker of their children, or a combination of the two. Mothers have more choices today than they had in the 1950s, when a woman with ambition was an embarrassment to her husband.

But what is the *right* choice? What *should* a mother do to ensure herself and her family happiness, success, and unity? A brief look at history will help us understand how we got to where we are today.

Since the early settlers came to the United States, the entire family worked together to produce food, weave textiles, make soap, prepare meals, and dip candles. The family was a unified team in producing goods for consumption. Public and private lives were intertwined. The mother was in charge of keeping the household well supplied and functioning, while the father's responsibilities were finances and the education of the children. Both sexes had demanding jobs.

But in the mid-1800s, with the coming of the Industrial Revolution, roles shifted. Fathers went to work in the factories, while mothers continued to stay home and run the household. Mothers no longer needed to use their minds to produce goods for the home, as these items were now manufactured and easily purchased. A mother still had household responsibilities, however, which became routinized and filled her time, but not necessarily her brain.

During World War II, millions of women were forced to move into factories to produce goods necessary for war. Mom became mother, father, *and* breadwinner. Having experienced being out in the workforce, women realized their potential beyond the home and family.

When the war ended and Dad came home from overseas, Mom was fired from the factories to make room for "the man of the family." It was at this point that the role of a "full-time" mother as a consumer rather than a producer peaked. During this boom in the 1950s, suburban housing blossomed. Mothers became isolated by housing patterns and her days spent chauffeuring other members of the family. These changes made her appear, at times, more like a servant to the family than an integral part of it.[1]

Most Americans believe that the 1950s lifestyle was the "norm," with Dad working to support the family, while Mom cared for the children in a spotlessly clean home with fresh-baked cookies. Yet this so-called norm developed because television shows such as *Leave It to Beaver* and *Father Knows Best* rose in popularity and replayed over the next forty years, equating families with breadwinner dads and stay-at-home moms.

When Betty Friedan, founder of the National Organization for Women, wrote *The Feminine Mystique* in 1963, she identified the voice within the suburban housewife: "I want something more than my husband and my children and my home."[2] Women married later and had fewer children. More and more women were college graduates moving into careers and had husbands who were no longer embarrassed by a working wife.

As Leora Tanebaum, author of books on women's issues, states in *Catfight: Women and Competition*, "[F]rom that point, the 1950's-era ideal family continued to live on only televised images. Nostalgia for the nuclear family as it was depicted in these shows has anxiety that the traditional nuclear family is the only correct and healthy type of family arrangement: When mothers work, the nostalgic-minded believe, families (and society) suffer."[3] This is where the Wall's foundation started, with society pressuring mothers to be June Cleaver, the gold standard in mothering, from *Leave It to Beaver*.

Yet the women's movement in the late 1960s and the 1970s frowned on women at home. Why were they not using their college degrees? Why were they depending on a man to provide for them? Cokie Roberts, news analyst for National Public Radio and ABC News, claims in her book, *We Are Our Mother's Daughters*, "The women's movement gave lip service to the concept of choice but didn't mean it. The strong message: Women, to have any worth, you must go to work, show that you are just like a man."[4] In the 1960s, employed mothers were on the defensive; in the 1970s stay-at-home mothers were on the defensive; by the time the 1980s rolled around, *everyone* was defensive.

In the 1980s and 1990s, expectations for women were elevated. But while women were now out in the workforce in large numbers, they were still doing 84 percent of the housework.[5] Mothers now had two jobs instead of one!

According to Shari Thurer, author of *The Myths of Motherhood: How Culture Reinvents the Good Mother*,

> Thirty years after Friedan, many women are on the edge of a huge generational divide, and they are experiencing vertigo. We are the first cohort of women, who, whether by choice or necessity, work outside the home. We are the first generation of women among many who dare to be ambitious. But there is no getting around the fact that ambition is not a maternal trait. Motherhood and ambition are still largely seen as opposing forces. More strangely expressed, a lack of ambition—or professed lack of ambition, a sacrificial willingness to set personal ambition aside—is still the virtuous proof of good mothering. For many women, perhaps most, motherhood versus personal ambition represents the heart of the feminine dilemma.[6]

So we had feminists breaking taboos by discussing the boredom and isolation of being confined to the home, and we also had mothers at home enjoying their lives who felt insulted and ridiculed. Neither the liberated, employed mother nor the traditional at-home mom was comfortable; each believed that society was damning her. This tension between the baby boomer mothers was labeled the "Mommy Wars" in the late 1980s by Jan Russell: "Working moms think stay-at-home moms are idle and self indulgent, stay-at-home moms think working moms are neglectful and egotistical."[7] After this was published, articles on this topic flooded newspapers and magazines. The debate over who is the better mother has raged since then.

"If we stay home, we fear that we are turning into our own mothers, complete with their low self status, self sacrifices, and frustrations. . . . But if we are ambitious, or even if we work outside our homes out of necessity, we are afraid of what our distraction will do to our children. . . . So where does this leave us? Either childless or very mixed up," claims Thurer.[8]

What should a mother do? Stay home with our low self-esteem and take comfort in the thought that we are the best mothers because we sacrifice for our children? Or continue to work and support our families while being tortured by thoughts of what we might be doing to our children by not being continuously at their sides? The choices that were meant to liberate women actually built a Wall between those on each side of the equation.

This book explores that Wall.

NOTES

1. Glenna Matthews, *Just a Housewife: The Rise and Fall of Domesticity in America* (New York: Oxford Press, 1987), p. 212.

2. Betty Friedan, *The Feminine Mystique* (New York: W. W. Norton, 1963), p. 323.

3. Leora Tanebaum, *Catfight: Women and Competition* (New York: Seven Stories Press, 2002), p. 258.

4. Cokie Roberts, *We Are Our Mothers' Daughters* (New York: William Morrow, 1998), p. 187.

5. Shari L. Thurer, *The Myths of Motherhood: How Culture Reinvents the Good Mother* (New York: Houghton Mifflin, 1994), p. 287.

6. Ibid.

7. Iris Krasnow, "It's Time to End the 'Mommy Wars,'" *Washington Post* (May 7, 1999): C5.

8. Thurer, *Myths of Motherhood*, p. 288.

ONE

IS THERE A WALL?

What do you do all day? versus How can you leave your children?

"When people learn that I am a stay-at-home mother, they start on bland subjects. They don't probe for depth—I have to lay it out for myself," declares North Carolinian Sally. "I definitely see the Wall. When people ask, 'What do you do?' the question makes me feel so small; that Wall comes right up. Working moms feel superior to me; they turn away from me as if I cannot possibly have a brain or anything interesting to say. They make me feel like I have nothing to contribute just because I am not punching a time clock. I work— I just don't get paid for it. I raise twins."

But Alison, a Connecticut marketing consultant, has a different take. "When at-home mothers find out that I work, a switch flips. People feel sorry for me and say, 'Oh, you poor thing, you work.' Others do not understand, saying, 'How long do you have to do that?' The Wall is most apparent when women find out for the first time that I am working—the warmth instantly goes away. Ninety-nine percent of them never even ask what I do."

Is there a tension, a conflict, a Wall between stay-at-home and employed mothers? Do employed mothers think that moms who stay home are lazy and dull? Do at-home mothers view employed moms as cold and neglectful toward their children?

"It is not an invisible Wall; it is an economic and lifestyle choice. Some people say they 'must' work for a high-spending lifestyle when they really don't have to. It is an economic decision, not an 'I must put food on the table' decision. They just want more money. It is the difference between two professionals, such as a doctor and a lawyer, versus two teachers who must both work to put food on the table," says Betty, a New Jersey stay-at-home mom. "It's very clear which parents are working for self-gratification versus the ones working to pay the bills. It irks me. My sister-in-law works full time to buy each of her kids six pairs of shoes. She really doesn't need to work and she keeps asking *me* when I will go back to my previous occupation."

Cristine, a Chicago cardiovascular trainer, makes other assertions. "At-home mothers have no energy for worldly discussions—these people aren't out in the world. Their subjects of conversation are children and menopause. They shut off their intellectual side. When I attempt to broach other subjects, I get into three sentences, and then their eyes glaze over."

"The attitude of the PTA moms is 'I don't have to work as my husband makes enough money for my family to live on.' They are a smug bunch of women. They don't say this to my face, but I really feel it along with the other full-time employed moms," claims Jamie, an insurance agent from Dallas.

THE WALL

After discussing this topic with over one hundred mothers, I can definitely say that a Wall exists between full-time employed and stay-at-home moms. A large majority of mothers, 80 percent of those interviewed, not only believe that there is a Wall but also claim to have experienced it themselves. In fact, more than half of the women discuss the Wall with spite, vengefulness, and scorn.

As the first women gained headway in the workplace in the 1960s and 1970s, many mothers took sides based on their choice, as employment for mothers was new and a major shift in society. But today, after thirty-five to forty years of women solidly establishing themselves in the marketplace; with over fifty percent of mothers being employed, most out of necessity; and with at-home mothers *choosing* to leave the workplace—rather than having no other option as in the 1950s—why would this Wall continue to exist? When I started asking other women about this, I heard all kinds of insinuations from both sides.

"I really don't fit in with the Junior League because the women who don't work outside the home feel that their status is better than mine," declares Melissa, vice president of business development with a New York Fortune 100 company. "My town can be very hoity-toity. The Junior League women said to me, 'I don't have to work, it's too bad that you work'; 'Oh, you still have to work?' My husband is not employed as he sold his business, making a great profit, but everyone assumes that I *have* to earn the household income since my husband stays home. If women don't have a good self-worth, then they have a problem with career women."

According to Tennessee at-home mother Patty, "At wine tastings with couples on Saturday night, I get the 'meet, greet, and turn.' New people that I am being introduced to say, 'Hello, my name is so and so, I work at XYZ corporation, what do you do?' The minute I mention that I'm a stay-at-home mother, the polite ones quickly claim that they need more wine and walk away, while the rude ones simply turn away, leaving me there alone with no excuses."

BUILDING THE FOUNDATION FOR THE WALL

When women finish their education—through high school, college, or graduate programs—they embark into chosen vocations and careers. Some become freelance artists, social workers, project engineers, physicians, or factory workers, while others become dieticians, lawyers, secretaries, chemists, sales representatives, or journalists. Some get married and start a family right away, and others wait years before looking for a spouse and having offspring. But no matter when women have children, a majority initially continue their jobs, exemplified by 99 percent of the women interviewed keeping their jobs when their children were first born.

The decision to remain working full time outside the home upon birthing children is simple for most women—they just need the money. Then one day, four-year-old Ashley comes home from daycare crying, the relative sitting Johnnie can no longer fulfill his needs as he begins to talk, the fourth nanny quits on Sally's second birthday, or Mommy is simply burned out and cannot carry on for one more day. For whatever reason, at this point, many mothers pull out of the workforce, stop their professional lives for the time being, and decide to stay home full time. This tends to occur when the children are under age five.[1]

To decide to stay home, to give up all that one has achieved, is a difficult task: less money, but more time with the children—less empowerment, less independence, but more nurturing, more special moments together.

Anne Crittenden, author of *The Price of Motherhood: Why the Most Important Job in the World Is Still the Least Valued,* claims, "To most women choice is all about bad options and difficult decisions: your children or your profession; taking on domestic chores or marital strife; a good night's sleep or time with your child; food on the table or your baby's safety; your right arm or your left."[2] The Wall's foundation is built because of today's cultural conflicts—society expects women to be full-fledged, paid participants *and* selfless mothers as well.

"I had empowerment. I dressed well, sat at a computer, was in a 'meet and greet' environment, traveled to Europe, negotiated billon-dollar deals, and was positioned to take on more responsibility. Yet I still felt that I was missing out: missing the first steps in walking, missing the first word. My heart isn't broken, but I did give these things up," says New Yorker Julie, former director of packaging at a large corporation. "Daycare was not great, as my children were crying when they came home each day. Then, as if their tears weren't enough, there is pressure in my neighborhood to be a stay-at-home mom because such great bonds exist between the women and children who are always participating in activities with one another. I was constantly thinking that I was sacrificing my *kids* for my *career*, compelling me to take a two-year leave of absence in order to really get to know my kids."

Resolving to continue with the career is an arduous decision. "Full-time employed mothers must be Herculean to meet all the goals—family, work, and relationships. I always feel guilty. I'm always afraid of something falling apart," says Elizabeth, director of human resources for an Ohio corporation.

Since choosing one lifestyle over another is so laborious, complicated, and emotionally charged, women tend to be extremely defensive of the side they have selected. They are validating their resolution, putting up their guard to protect their emotions, hence building the foundation for the Wall.

"Lots of stay-at-home moms are well educated and achievement oriented, bringing the same attributes to being a mother as they would to a career. They are very intense. They bring that same intensity into the home to validate their decision to vacate their offices for the sake of their children. To them the world becomes black and white because of their decision. Being an at-home mother is a good choice, and being a full-time working mom is a bad choice," believes Audrey, Pennsylvania university professor.

Margaret, an actuary from Atlantis, Florida, says, "As a working mother, I feel judged by stay-at-home moms, particularly when my job is perceived as more of a choice than an economic necessity. They're always throwing out barbs, letting me know how they're better mothers than I am since they're there to put a Band-Aid on their child's knee when they fall, and I'm not."

"People say, 'So you'll be going back to work when the kids get older.' I reply, 'No.' It's an insecurity on both sides. Relatives are constantly asking me when I'm going back to work, not believing my answer of 'never,'" asserts former banker Sara.

"There's a huge Wall between stay-at-home mothers and full-time working moms. I tried to fit in with the National Charity League, but the at-home moms have little cliques; Bunco groups are the same. As a full-time career mother, I didn't fit in at all," says Connecticut accountant Susan.

According to Kathy, vice president of operations in a family-owned St. Charles, Illinois, company, "A huge wall exists in my town. My sister wasn't included in church and neighborhood social activities because she worked full time, and the majority of the moms in town stay home. And to make matters worse, her children never played sports. She was ostracized so much that she had to set up a social life elsewhere."

"At-home mothers have coffees, and I attend whenever possible. One woman was going back to work, and when one of the mothers was toasting her, she said, 'Better her than me,' clearly defending her lifestyle. I don't talk about work with that group as I refuse to get into the nitty-gritty with them," claims St. Louis graphic designer Debbie.

But Nashville stay-at-home mother Nicole simply says, "I have hostility toward employed mothers who don't have to work to put food on the table."

"One friend had an issue with me going back to work and wouldn't look at me. She thought that we were best friends and I had let her down by returning to my profession," states Martha, a special education teacher from New Mexico.

Defensive, defensive, defensive—everyone is trying to defend her own position. No one thinks she is doing it *all* right, so each woman is justifying her own choice.

ERECTING THE WALL

NBC commentator Cokie Roberts claims that women make each other's existence tougher by forcing their lifestyle onto others.[3] By saying "my choice is the right choice," women became critical and sometimes even jealous of the other's decision. The criticisms begin to pull mothers apart from one another.

While the stay-at-home moms' superior parenting attitude makes the full-time career mother feel even more guilty about employment than she would otherwise, the career mom has professional bragging rights, making the at-home mother feel as though she has a dull mind. The stay-at-home and employed mothers' schedules are vastly different from one another, forming a time barrier and furthering the already numerous differences between the two groups. And these conflicts extend even to women within families, raging from sister to sister and mother to daughter.

When Tim McGuire, United Feature national syndicated columnist, penned a column regarding the tensions between employed and at-home mothers, the intolerance, vitriol, and scorn he found between the two groups surprised him.[4] All these attitudes, feelings, viewpoints, and disparities are the bricks building the Wall.

Superior Mothers

"In my neighborhood, almost all the mothers stay home, making me feel that I have more in common with the dads than the moms because I work outside the home. I can't converse with the men because it's an unwritten social rule in my area that women talk with women regarding mommy issues such as kids, school, et cetera. The at-home moms look at me as the 'bad mother' because I'm not staying home with my kids—I'm not doing what I should be. The stay-at-home moms will talk to me, but the conversations are stilted and they look at me through skeptical eyes," says Nancy, a New Jersey attorney. "I see a huge Wall between employed and at-home moms because mothers staying home say, 'I have sacrificed to be with my kids.' They're a bit self-righteous about being a good mom."

This is the payoff for retreating from the workplace, having more time, and, a mother hopes, a better relationship with her children than if she had continued working. Since most at-home mothers have surrendered income and a professional identity for the betterment of their children, they believe that they *must* be superior to full-time employed moms in order to justify their at-home status to themselves. This feeling of superiority in parenting skills heightens the Wall.

At-home mom Sally reveals, "I see career mothers in clubs, socially, and through volunteer work, but I don't interact with those who have a 'chip on their shoulder.' They are threatened by me, my bonds with my children, and insecure about their own choice. I don't express how I personally view staying home to be important. I won't go there with them, even if they press to get it out of me."

"I feel I can share troubles with raising my first child and getting kids ready in the morning with other full-time working women. I can't do that with stay-at-home mothers because they feel that I made the wrong moral decision and, therefore, am an inferior mother," claims marketing vice president Amy from Cupertino, California.

"The stay-at-home mothers running the PTA in my town design meetings in the mornings while children are at school, locking out full-time employed parents' participation. The implication is that career parents don't want to attend PTA meetings for their children because they aren't willing to make sacrifices for them," says insurance agent Jamie. "I resent the implication that my occupation makes me less of a loving, caring mother."

Jeanne, an Arkansas pharmacist, agrees. "An army of at-home mothers run the elementary school. They have parties and presentations during the day, making it difficult for employed parents to attend. It's challenging to go to when they are during the day, yet you are the 'bad mom' if you do not show up at these events."

Guilt of Working

"With my new job, I'm no longer working from home as I have been for the last ten years," claims church director Phyllis from San Ramon, California. "I feel as though I am abandoning my fourteen-year-old because of my long hours. Even though my husband and I juggle all the time to try to be at home as much as possible, the guilt is still there."

Full-time employed mothers already have enough conflicted internal feelings, so this sense of superiority radiating from stay-at-home mothers magnifies the guilt: the guilt of not knowing what her eighth grader is doing after school, the guilt of washing and ironing clothes at 8 p.m. rather than reading to her four-year-old, the guilt of serving fast food for dinner, the guilt of simply not being there. Many of these mothers would like to stay home with their children but just can't afford to.

"I know several career women whose children are raised by nannies as the parent surrogate," says Boulder, Colorado, mom Sheila. "They have lots of guilt and spend every weekend buying clothes and toys for their kids to compensate for not being around for them. The house is full of toys, but not of their mother's presence."

"I had a friend who took the day off of work to be with her children at a school party, yet none of the at-home mothers would talk to her. She felt that they were scorning her and the guilt was enormous," conveys Pamela. "Working full time was a career decision for her."

"When I wanted to co-host a kindergarten party, I let the classroom mothers know I could come as long as I had notice so that I could ensure I was not scheduled to be in court that day," says attorney Nancy. "One mom said, 'Boo, hoo, hoo! You work, oh, too bad! How long will you have to work for?' in a baby voice. It made me feel like a real loser as if I had made a bad choice, as though my family was financially in need, that we could not cut it in an affluent town."

"Sometimes I feel less than adequate as a mother because I spend less time with my kids than I would like," declares Spokane credit manager Sharon. "So is my guilt internal or from other mother's comments? If I act defensive, it turns other people off. Some ask, 'Why isn't your child in the church preschool?' I have to say, 'Because I am working, and they are in day-care.' They reply, 'Oh, that's too bad.' It's that kind of conditioning that makes me defensive."

Professional Bragging Rights

"I definitely agree with there being a Wall. . . . It's almost jealousy or envy that you, as an employed mother, have somewhere to go each day with stimulating conversation, while the stay-at-home mothers do not. All the moms that I know have chosen to be at home, making me feel as if I am the only mother at the office. I feel so isolated as a mother when I try to fit into the nonworking world," declares Jenny, sales representative at a large corporation in Illinois. "When you are with moms staying home, you don't brag that you work."

Women who hold full-time professions are proud they have a career yet believe that they are "boasting" about their vocations and opportunities to at-home moms when discussing their occupations. They believe that mothers at home have no interest in professional or occupational conversations, otherwise they would still be working in a chosen vocation.

"Stay-at-home moms have worked, but just jobs, not real careers. You sort people out by testing the waters, searching for women that you can connect with and build relationships with," claims Elizabeth, director of human resources. "Corporate career women have an air of confidence around them, which is intimidating to nonworking moms. You don't want to talk about your career because it makes them feel bad; you don't want to wear your master's degree over a coffee cup. You don't talk about these concepts we are discussing now—you would bore everyone. I try to meet stay-at-home mothers on their own terms."

Dull Minds

"Stay-at-home mothers' focus is narrowed, even if they were well versed prior to staying home; they have become narrow. They fall into a trap of a loss of perspective: they just see their home, their schools, their towns. They do not see the broader issues," says Connecticut finance manager Chris. "It's hard to find mutual interests between mothers in the workplace and ones staying home. You must adapt to audiences that you are with, and, let's face it, stay-at-home mothers are just not interesting. As a working mother, I start out discussing bland subjects. Women at home have chosen omission, to put their kids first and all else secondary."

Since at-home mothers do not initiate conversations about employed mothers' careers or vocations, they are seen as having dull minds by many working-out-of-the-home mothers. In fact, many employed mothers claim to "dumb down" their conversations with at-home mothers. One professional mother told me that "stay-at-home mothers cannot find their way out of a paper bag." No wonder there is a Wall between these groups.

"When at family gatherings, everyone asks my sister-in-law, 'How's the job?' Yet no one asks me what I am doing. I am doing a lot!" claims Greenville, South Carolina, at-home mom Diane. "Working women don't engage stay-at-home women because they are afraid that you don't do anything except watch soap operas all day, even though you have a full life within your community, children's schools, and church."

"It is a waste of resources for well-educated women to stay home with kids. If they put their energy into the community, such as the temple, it's terrific, but those who just get manicures, decorate the house, and work out are wasting their education and letting their minds go," says actuary Margaret.

"When I am in social settings and I state that I'm an at-home mother, all conversations stop. It is amazing to me that people are so shortsighted to think that staying home makes women brain-dead. In fact, I hit the Wall so often that I used to cut out magazine and newspaper articles on why it was 'us' versus 'them,'" reveals former banker Dawn. "I think that people don't know what to say to at-home moms. My own mother stayed home and used to read the newspaper all of the time to be up on current events. She was always ready to talk about them as a defense mechanism for this. I must admit, I do the same thing so I have something to talk about on social occasions."

"I have heard career moms refer to my Web designing and say, 'You really need to do something with this.' But I *am* doing something with it— I'm working five hours per week. I am doing this on my own terms as I wasn't around with my son in early years and do *not* want to go back to full-time work," says Natalie from Portland, Oregon.

Time Barrier

"I socialize with at-home mothers because that is who is available during the day. I'm done socializing when my family comes home because I want to be with them—that's why I stayed home in the first place. This is what keeps me separated from professional mothers," says Patty, a former secretary.

Again and again, time came up in conversations regarding the Wall. All the mothers interviewed noted that it is hard to be friends with women whose schedules and attitudes are so drastically different from their own. The at-home mother does her grocery shopping, errands, and socializing with her friends while the children are in school during the week so that she can focus on her children and husband when they get home at night and on weekends. Full-time employed moms, however, catch up with their chores, shopping, and mingling with their friends on the weekends when at-home mothers are focusing on their families.

According to stay-at-home mom Betty, "Full-time employed mothers aren't friends with at-home moms around here in New Jersey because their availability is different. At-home mothers don't make phone calls or plans to be with friends when Dad is home on weekends—that's family time. Yet that's when career moms are available. Therefore, at-home and employed moms' schedules are totally out of sync. And, as we all know, career mothers can't have lots of friends anyway, as they have no time."

"It is harder to get together with at-home mothers," says Melissa, a New York vice president. "One friend will meet me for lunch by my office, but she is unusual in that respect. I meet at-home moms through the kids, but these friends aren't as close as the other working mothers."

"It is hard to continue friendships with working mothers because they don't have free time," says at-home mom Diane. "So a barrier has developed based on schedule differences alone. Some of my working friends think that I have copped out, but I think that they are jealous that I can stay home."

Sister versus Sister

Initially, I hypothesized that the Wall existed only between strangers, people who don't know each other well and, therefore, tend to stereotype one another. I assumed that *strangers* constructed the Wall. But I was wrong. Many of the women interviewed actually have their biggest Walls built between family members—sisters, mothers, and/or sisters-in-law. One woman maintains an occupation, while the relation stays home, and neither sees nor understands the other one's side.

"My mother worked outside the home, but my sister, Claire, and her daughters stay home. If something goes wrong with my children or my life in general, Claire thinks it's due to my being a professional mother," states Jennifer, a Colorado psychiatrist. "When my daughter was sick with cancer, I stopped working for a year to tend to her needs and illness. Claire said that it was 'really good' to see me overcome my own needs to tend to my sick daughter. I was appalled at her insinuations."

"My sister, Candace, wants to be an equal partner with her husband, never letting him 'one up' her in his career. Yet her children have no consistency in their lives as they are constantly shuffled from nannies to sitters back to nannies, resulting in them being wild and undisciplined," says at-home mother Jo Ann. "But my sister's house, unlike her children, is perfect. Nothing is ever out of place."

She adds, "We are on opposite sides of the fence. Candace's husband said that he would not give me any spending money if he were my husband, Ted, because I am not pulling my weight. Candace's husband doesn't realize that Ted succeeds in his career because *I* do everything regarding the home and family. *I* pay the bills, *I* do the laundry, *I* mow the lawn, *I* clean, *I* cook, *I* repair broken items in the house. I pull my weight, not by earning a paycheck, but by organizing and caring for my home and children. Running the house is my job; all that I do is part of my job description. It makes Ted's life better, too, as he gets more time on the weekends with the kids because I have completed all the chores during the week. Candace's husband should do half of the housework, but he considers it beneath him. In Candace's house, there's lots of crying and screaming at night. The kids are tired and homework is not finished, even though it is 9 p.m. Laundry is done at 10 p.m. so everyone has something to wear the next day. My home is much calmer."

"My younger sister, Kathleen, didn't go to college. It's not in her chemistry to work," says Marcia, a Connecticut engineer. "She's a stay-at-home mother with a husband who has a high-pressure job, making her stressed out. Even though Kathleen volunteers in several areas, including the schools and her town library, we still avoid talking about work as it is a sore subject with her. I feel that I must prove to Kathleen that I spend quality time with my daughter because she can make me feel non-nurturing and guilty as a mother. And she tries to prove to *me* that she is not the 'barefoot and pregnant' housewife, that she has an important life."

HOW BIG AND HOW HIGH?

While it is clear that the Wall exists today, it is not obvious how pervasive it is. Does the Wall cross different age groups? Is it felt in all areas across the country? And to what degree is it felt? The next chapter investigates who experiences the barrier and how much of it they feel.

NOTES

1. Based on interviews.

2. Ann Crittenden, *The Price of Motherhood: Why the Most Important Job in the World Is Still the Least Valued* (New York: Henry Holt, 2001), p. 237.

3. Cokie Roberts, *We Are Our Mothers' Daughters* (New York: William Morrow, 1998), p. 186.

4. Tim McGuire, "Women Can Find Meaning at Home as Well as at Work," *St. Louis Post-Dispatch* (March 8, 2004): C1.

TWO

THE DYNAMICS OF THE WALL

"There is a huge wall. I believe neither is supporting the other."

Are mothers standing beside one another, championing each other's causes? Or do they denigrate and belittle the "other" side? How do the following comments sound to you?

"Stay-at-home moms are too stupid to realize that their brains are turning to mush," claims Floridian actuary Margaret.

"Mothers at home have better relationships with their husbands than full-time employed mothers," asserts former environmental engineer Tracy. "The working out-of-the-house moms feel dumped on, while their spouses feel as though they are always being nagged, with lots of bickering going on. Career women are envious of the calm, put-together life of at-home mothers. There's jealousy and a sense of being critical between those who work full time versus those who stay home."

"Stay-at-home mothers' eyes bore into me at school events," says Jeanne, a pharmacist. "They're practically saying to me, 'You don't love your children; you are selfish.' I want to ask them, 'Why did you go to graduate school?' I feel that they threw in the towel, and I almost view them with sympathy."

Eighty percent of the women interviewed sense the Wall, feeling that the woman on the "other side" is not supporting her. Yet every mother who perceives the Wall does not sense it in the same way. The level of intolerance, vehemence, and intensity of feelings vary from mother to mother. I describe these levels of feelings as the height of the Wall. The more intense the perception of the Wall is, the higher the Wall is built. If a mother has sensed the Wall only once or twice in passing and barely noticed it, then the Wall is very low for her. If, however, a mother has telephone arguments weekly with her mother-in-law regarding her choice of employment versus staying home, the Wall is extremely high.

THE WALL BETWEEN WOMEN

The Wall's height can range from virtually nonexistent to extremely high based on several factors, such as the age of one's children, a woman's level of education, internal conflict, what area of the country a mother lives in, or whom a mother has as friends. By analyzing the dynamics of the Wall, I found that the largest factor in determining its height is the age of a woman's children.

CHILDREN'S AGE DIFFERENCE

The Wall is highest when children are young, particularly when they are in elementary school. When the children are under age four, many mothers are undecided and torn between employment or staying home. Do they have enough financial stability to stay home? Do they want to remain employed? If they stay home for a few years, will they regret it when they reenter the workforce? Will they regret it if they *don't* stay home with their children when they are young?

The Wall is apparent in a mother's interaction with neighbors or relatives, but it is not at its peak, as indecision is still in many mothers' minds. But by the time their children are in elementary school, most mothers have chosen their position. Moreover, until children enter kindergarten, mothers generally are interacting with others just like themselves. Nursery schools and prekindergarten classes are either blended with full-time daycare for employed mothers or geared for stay-at-home moms, running half-day sessions. Once children enter kindergarten, however, all types of mothers meet through the elementary schools. This is where the Wall reaches its peak. Women have chosen sides—now they are meeting those in the opposite camp and must defend their decision in order to avert remorse.

"Working mothers had warned me, but I never saw it until my children were elementary school age," says Ronnie, director of procurement. "When my child entered kindergarten, a woman stopped me in the hallway of my workplace asking if Chantilly was my child. When I said yes, she said that our children were attending the same school, but in different classes. She asked me how it felt to be the only working mother in my child's class. This was news to me, and when I asked her how she learned of this, she replied that a neighbor had told her. I was mortified that people were talking about me. Now, at elementary school events, I get those 'why did you have children if you are not at home with them' glares. Like I said, I *was* warned but not mentally prepared for these strong reactions."

Kim, a part-time office manager from Missouri, adds, "In the past, I stayed involved with the kids in school and worked part-time, having a foot in both worlds, so I was accepted by all groups of women. If I had been employed full time and not participated in the schools, the Wall would have been extremely high with my neighbors, making life at home very uncomfortable."

Then, as children age, entering middle school and high school, they become more self-sufficient. And as the children become more independent, stay-at-home mothers are free to pursue personal interests, presenting an opportunity to form a personal identity beyond "Mom." This issue of developing and maintaining an identity beyond motherhood enables at-home mothers to become either more open to employed mothers or, perhaps, even employed themselves, causing a lowering of the Wall.

"I talked to one at-home mom who really wanted to hold a conversation regarding my job. I got the impression that she was envious, as she said that she dreams about the day that she can go back to her former career when her children are old enough to handle themselves," asserts Lynn, Olympic Committee adviser.

Employed mothers realize during their sons' and daughters' middle and high school years that their children are rapidly approaching college and adulthood, causing moms to reschedule their lives to make more time for their teenagers or to realize that maybe, just maybe, they have missed something by being at the office. This lowers the Wall from their side as well.

"Working is an integral part of me—it's how I identify myself after twenty years of employment," states Mary, owner of a photography studio in Great Bend, Kansas. "Yet I might not mind stopping work now that my daughter is maturing, triggering thoughts of my own mortality outside of work, influencing my decision to consider selling the studio. As you age, you lose your capabilities to do things, and I want to travel, hike, and become an advocate for the environment before I can't. I'm starting to think that it's not that far off."

So the Wall lowers from both sides over time. It never disappears, but the attitudes of the two dissimilar types of mothers are beginning to converge. As stay-at-home mother Rachael says, "When my children were little, there was more of a Wall, but as my children and their friends grow, entering high school, I see many of my at-home friends considering part-time and full-time employment."

Anne, a vice president of a California promotional corporation and the breadwinner for her family, adds, "I'm approaching fifty and thinking of college and Zach, my son, leaving the nest. I have become reflective as my parents recently died, and mortality is setting in. In the past, I got a kick out of making a great presentation or landing a new client, but that is not as important to me anymore. My world is Zach and my husband, Adam, now. I want to be part of Zach's life and would love to be at home, but must go to the office to support all of us. I wonder if you had asked me these questions ten years ago if I would have answered them differently."

Rachael's and Anne's comments sync well with a study done for Euro RSCG Worldwide, an advertising agency, stating that the "parent" label grows more important with age. While 62 percent of the respondents ages eighteen to thirty-four felt that the label "mother" or "father" was fundamental to their identity, the percentage rose to 80 percent when the respondents were in the thirty-five-to-fifty age group.[1]

Based on these comments, I expected to find a correlation that the older a mother is, the lower the Wall is. While the age of the mother is somewhat important, the real factor ties to the age of her children. A thirty-nine-year-old mother with a five-year-old daughter is as adamant about the Wall as a twenty-seven-year-old mother with a five-year-old son. The child's age is the driving factor.

According to North Carolinian Corey, "When my kids were small, I thought that *all* moms should stay at home, clearly holding the 'stay-at-home mom' mind-set as all my friends were at home. But now, I'm changing my view as I'm aging, seeing excellent reasons to maintain a career. Some women toiled to receive a good education and practically broke their backs to reach their high-level positions prior to having children. I can now see why they would not want to give that up, but I did *not* recognize it when my kids were toddlers."

EDUCATION

Cindy, a part-time banker, voluntarily brought up the subject of education. "My mother-in-law, Wilma, said to me that the reason there is a Wall is because women are so overeducated today. Wilma claims if women receive less education, not obtaining the master's and doctorate degrees, we would be much happier as mothers. That made me so mad! She told me it was my credentials that led to my dissatisfaction in my life at home, and if I didn't know better, then I wouldn't be so frustrated at home. This was a direct attack on me."

In actuality, Wilma was dead wrong. The more education women have, the lower the Wall. Every mother interviewed who had a high school diploma as her highest level of education experienced the Wall, yet not one mother with a PhD did. Mothers with doctorates had heard of the Wall but never felt it themselves. About one-sixth of the mothers with an undergraduate degree never sensed the Wall, while approximately one-third of those with a master's degree did not experience it. While the majority of mothers, regardless of their education, feel the Wall, their sensitivity to the Wall decreases as their level of education increases.

Why is this true? Based on these mothers' comments, part of the reason is the more education a woman receives, the higher the likelihood that she will be employed. The higher the likelihood that she is employed, the higher the chances that she simply *doesn't interact* with stay-at-home mothers, and, therefore, she *can't* experience the Wall. As Pamela, a Chicago resident with an MBA, says, "It is an inadvertent result of circumstances. The structure of everyone's lives is the biggest barrier between women."

Lynn, the Olympics Committee adviser, agrees. "There's little opportunity between full-time employed and at-home moms to interact. You can't be at the park in the afternoons when you have a career demanding your presence at the office. There's a lack of opportunities for connection. I never established at-home friends until I began working part-time."

So part of the reason these few mothers don't sense the Wall is their paths don't cross with mothers in dissimilar situations. It's not a conscious action—it's just like mothers of girls knowing primarily the girls' moms and mothers of boys knowing primarily the boys' moms.

Another hypothesis for the decrease in sensitivity to the Wall as level of education increases is that self-confidence and openness to new ideas emerge as women attain higher levels of education. Advanced education teaches women to look at many sides of a situation before making decisions, which may result in the lowering of the Wall. Having an advanced degree also gives women high self-esteem and self-assurance, which aids them in being more accepting of others who hold opinions that differ greatly from their own.

"I see a Wall with those who married right out of high school. They are more judgmental than women who have worked professionally for ten years, even though both groups are stay-at-home moms now. I get flak from within my own family because they say that I'm not willing to sacrifice for my own children, that I'm into my own thing. But none of them held professional occupations while they were waiting to have children, just short-term jobs. There's definitely a Wall there," says Laura, a hospital administrative assistant.

INTERNAL CONFLICT

Of the women interviewed, a few questioned whether it is internal guilt that makes them defensive rather than the dissimilar mothers themselves. Because most at-home moms had a career and chose to abandon it, are they feeling guilty about being *able* to stay home? Do they feel guilty that they *can* enjoy their children, while their husbands shoulder the financial obligations? And on the other side, do the full-time working mothers yearn to *be* at home? Do they question their *own* decision to continue in the workforce and how that affects their relationship with their children?

Several former professionals—intelligent, successful, and interesting— had no idea that they would turn into at-home mothers. They talked to me about internal conflict, about staying home. They discussed the pros and cons—less money to spend but more time with each child, fewer self-accomplishments but a smoother-running household, a lack of identity beyond "mommy" but an increased quality in family lifestyle. They would *rather* be at work facing intellectual challenges but believe that they *should* be home raising the children.

"I don't know if employed mothers are making me feel this way or I'm feeling it from the inside, but I feel less as a person because I no longer have a career. I have to justify my life each day when I am not at the office. Is this coming from within me, or it is from them? I don't know," says at-home mother and former sports medical expert Nicole.

Special education teacher Martha says, "As a working mom, I feel comfortable with stay-at-home mothers, but *they* are uncomfortable with their status versus mine. They feel they need to justify themselves because they think that I am looking down on them, even though I'm not."

Career-oriented mothers also talked about their internal conflict. While these women gain fulfillment and self-esteem from their occupations, their internal struggle arises from a lack of time available for their sons and daughters, from a sense of inadequacy as mothers, and from daily compromises made between the office and home.

According to commodity trader Barbara, "My own perception is that at-home moms do not look down their noses at me, but their very presence makes me feel guilty. They make me think that if I was a stay-at-home mother, maybe my kids would have better manners, maybe my kids would brush their teeth more."

"Five of us mothers birthed together within a six-month period," says Susan, a Connecticut accountant. "Since the other four decided to leave work and I didn't, I felt a big disconnect from them, even though they were my best friends. I was creating my own Wall because of my own issues. *I* was the insecure one, tortured and torn, not them. I felt that maybe there was something to what people were saying about children needing their mothers at home. . . . You have an obligation to fulfill, you have guilt. You want to be successful, independent, and self-sufficient, but not to the detriment of your children. Eighty percent of the Wall is from within me and twenty percent from the outside."

One-third of the mothers interviewed revealed this internal conflict. It transcends age, region of the country, and education. Women from both sides feel internal uncertainty about their decisions and curiosity regarding how life might have been had they followed another path.

REGIONALIZATION

Although 80 percent of mothers interviewed have felt the Wall, it isn't perceived equally across the country as there are regional differences. In the Southeast, the Wall is higher, felt more strongly than in the rest of the country. This could be attributed to stronger religious ties, hence, a traditional outlook, as more mothers here mentioned church or synagogue memberships and activities than in any other section of the country. In addition, the Southeast is more conservative than other areas and would, therefore, have a stronger bias toward viewing "good mothers" as the ones who stay home with their children.

"I worked while I was young and held off having kids until I was in my thirties. It is difficult to imagine working today the way I did before having kids and then rushing home to attend to children. So I made the choice to stop and enjoy my children," says Holly, a Southern stay-at-home mom and former documentation manager. "I have had that 'rush, rush' life and wanted to ease up, savoring each day a little bit more. It seems that Southern moms like slowing down and enjoying life, while Northern moms appear to feel more guilt about cutting back and staying home."

On the West Coast, however, the Wall is weaker because it is felt by a lower percentage of mothers versus the norm for the country. Discussing why this might be true with women from California and Oregon, I came up with two hypothetical factors. The first one is the extreme high cost of living, necessitating more mothers to seek employment than in other parts of the country. In fact, many of the West Coast mothers interviewed didn't even know *any* moms who were not employed either full time or part time.

Irisa explains, "In California, people don't criticize you for paying your mortgage, as the cost of housing is astronomical. What you get for three-quarters of a million dollars here would be a third of that in other parts of the country. I have seen some homes for one and half million dollars that are absolute dumps, so mothers do not criticize each other for employment because they understand the cost of a decent home. Living in California, you must pay the price. Most can't afford to be at-home moms here because of that and are actually moving to other states where housing is a lot less expensive. Those who are stay-at-home mothers here are in very humble circumstances unless their husbands made millions in the dot-com explosion."

Second, the West Coast has a laid-back attitude about life versus the remainder of the country. Its population focuses on quality of lifestyle and health, ensuring that daily pursuits include a mix of hiking, painting, bicycling, or other activities of enjoyment more than do populations in other parts of the country. This results in people on the West Coast holding a less intense attitude regarding employment than those on the East Coast. The West Coast's mantra is closer to "Life is to be enjoyed" than the East Coast's of "Business is first and foremost," whether business is employment or volunteer work.

And while the majority of women on the West Coast did perceive the Wall, their overall attitude was not as vehement, forceful, or intense and was much more accepting of one another than in other sections of the country. The more I discussed the topic with women on the West Coast, the more they voluntarily brought up the subject of wanting more of a balance for all mothers. This was unlike the case in the Northeast or Southeast as women in both of these regions were unshakable in their opinions, making statements such as, "I have little regard for full-time-career mothers who work for any reason other than to put food on the table." Because West Coast women are more understanding and empathetic of women on the other side of the Wall from themselves, they are lowering the Wall and initiating its demolition.

SOCIALIZING WITH COLLEAGUES

Because there is envy and misunderstanding between both sides, many women tend to socialize mainly with mothers who have made the same life decision. A third of the women who have not experienced the Wall socialize only with women who have chosen a similar path. Sometimes these two types of women never encounter one another in their daily lives.

"All the women at my office are mothers. We move in a social circle through my children's daycare, where all the other parents are also dual-career couples, never interacting with stay-at-home mothers. So I don't feel the Wall. I have a social circle where my family fits in well. . . . It helps us as a family," says chemical engineer Marcia.

DOES IT HAVE TO EXIST?

"Unfortunately, I feel that the Wall between out-of-the-home-working and stay-at-home women will always be there. Although I can understand how difficult it must be to go to work all day and then come home trying to do everything else, only a woman who has been in a stay-at-home position understands what being 'at-home' truly entails," says Emily.

Marketing consultant Alison agrees. "There's no desire in either camp to fix it. Employed mothers can live in a world independent of moms at home—you run in the circle that you run in. I have no idea what stay-at-home mothers do all day. I see people walking their dogs, exercising at the fitness clubs, but I never dwell on the other side of life."

I don't agree with this assessment. In fact, by discussing this topic with over one hundred women, I have listened to opinions and heard of actions that show some women are already moving in the direction of tearing down the Wall, as depicted by several of the women living on the West Coast.

THE WALL BETWEEN WOMEN

To rid ourselves of the Wall, we must first understand each other by breaking through the stereotypes and putting ourselves in each other's shoes. In order to shatter these clichés, we must stand up and recognize what stereotypes we are assigning to each other. This sounds simple yet is actually difficult to do. Let's look at the myths we have conjured up regarding one another.

NOTE

1. Market Probe International, "Prosumer Pulse2004: A Global Study—Anticipating Consumer Demand," Conducted for EuroRSCG Worldwide (February 2004), Education and Parenting, p. 3.

THREE

THE STEREOTYPES: MYTHS OR REALITY?

"Her child is like the second house at the beach" versus "She is a slob wearing sweatpants, with yogurt on her shirt, watching *Oprah*."

"**A**t-home mothers feel that full-time employed moms are not involved enough with their children, not supporting them at school-wide sports days or attending special, individual presentations in the classroom. Stay-at-home mothers feel that they carry the load of volunteer work in the schools. In addition, these mothers feel that it is unfair to force children to attend before *and* after school programs. They believe that these dual-career parents have made bad choices," asserts Katie, a part-time emergency planner from San Francisco. "On the other hand, full-time employed moms think that at-home mothers have lots of free time on their hands. Professional moms can't fathom how mothers staying home can be busy all day. They don't see these at-home women as a productive part of society. When they see the at-home mothers in the classrooms, they say to themselves, 'Why not? What else do these women have to do?' They have no idea how busy they are."

Women—we do it to ourselves on both sides. By looking at the current stereotypes, we can see how these two groups of women have a hard time understanding each another. All the images in this chapter were obtained from the women interviewed. While several admitted that these are exaggerated illustrations, others felt that these stereotypes are realistic. The following descriptions were top of mind for them, and as stereotypes go, they are not flattering for anyone.

THE EMPLOYED MOTHER

The employed mother's imagery is broken into two distinct groups. The first type is the driven, ambitious achiever—she is the "professional" who "chose" a career rather than "has" to work. The second type is the middle-class woman who struggles to make ends meet, the "harried soul." Both types have characteristics in common, such as being emotionally stressed out and considered "sloppy" mothers by those staying at home, but they are seen as dissimilar people and are given sympathy accordingly.

The "Professional"

This is the high-powered professional woman who wears a suit, with the briefcase in one arm and a child in the other as she pushes her grocery cart through the store. She is professional, successful, confident, and intelligent. Others see her as highly motivated and well educated. She is driven; she is ambitious; she is stylishly dressed; she is full of energy; she is dynamic; she is a high achiever, making things happen in the world. This woman has a fabulous career and makes no apologies about it. Her financial status gives her respect among adults. She gives the illusion of doing it all—she is great at her job, a gourmet chef, and a superb hostess and appears to relate well to her children.

But she is also cold, uncaring, and power hungry. She is self-centered and materialistic. She is someone who claims to do it all but really pays someone else to do it for her. Feeding her family fast food for dinner, she is blind to what she is missing with her children, and they are falling by the wayside. Her wants are prioritized over her family's needs, with the children coming in second and being raised by someone else. Her career is more important to her than the kids. People cock an eyebrow at her because, to sum it up, she is seen as selfish, running with the jet-setters and living in the fast lane.

The "Harried Soul"

Here is the middle-class woman who helps keep a roof over the family's heads and food on the table. She has to work and isn't necessarily happy about it, preferring to stay home. With too much on her plate, she is overextended. While acting as the best mother possible under the circumstances, she comes up short more often than not whenever the kids are concerned. This woman can be either a professional, such as nurse, banker, or lawyer, or a nonprofessional, such an artist or beautician. She is a harried soul, torn in many directions.

Both the "harried soul" and the "professional" are emotionally and physically stressed out. They are overwhelmed and, therefore, seen as out-of-control, sloppy mothers who do not RSVP, send no thank-yous, and put a ten- or twenty-dollar bill in a card as a birthday present instead of sending a gift. They appear as never being around for their children. Different jobs, however, induce dissimilar reactions. If one is a female executive making $600,000 in the Chrysler Building, she receives no empathy, but if she *cleans* the Chrysler Building for a vocation, she gets compassion. The stay-at-home counterparts wonder, "Oh, my God, how do you do it? How can you really know your kids and do it all?"

THE STAY-AT-HOME MOTHER

Just as full-time employed moms are put into two different categories, so are the stay-at-home mothers. One half of those interviewed, including some at-home mothers themselves, envision stay-at-home mothers as so "simple" that they are incapable of having an occupation—they are the first type. Conversely, the second type is the "hard-edged volunteer/socialite" who frequents the gym, runs the schools, and visits the nail salons, while her social life as well as her children's is top of mind at all times.

The "Simpleton"

She is defined by what she is not. She is not interesting, not highly motivated, and not smart. She is "simple." She is boring, dependent, insecure, limited, and incapable, clearly not an intellectual match for her spouse. "Overweight" and "wearing out-of-date clothing" describe her looks. In fact, she can't get out of her sweats. She secured a ring, caught her husband, and now she is done—she doesn't have to become anything more. She has no pressure to pull it together and may even be described as lazy. Her days are spent cooking and cleaning while watching soap operas religiously on television. Hence, she is a limited, dowdy, middle-age, Bunco-playing mom who is willing to put everyone else first.

But she does pour her heart and soul into her children, bringing freshly baked cookies or homemade orange juice popsicles into the backyard as a snack on a summer's day. She is warm, nurturing, and loving. She is the traditional, moral mother willing to shoulder the burden of the family. And while the world views her staying home with the children as a noble act of self-sacrifice, she is still seen as boring, passive, and certainly "not qualified to work outside the home."

The "Hard-Edged Volunteer/Socialite"

Driving a Suburban to the gym with a Starbucks cup in one hand and the steering wheel in the other, this at-home mother is very involved with her social engagements as well as her children's activities. This is the woman who could be employed but has chosen to stay home. Since her husband makes good money, she hires a maid and others to do her daily chores. Therefore, she needs to fill her life and so has a hard edge to her extremely aggressive volunteerism. This is the education advocate, the ultimate PTA mom. She schedules her children just as she would prepare a boardroom presentation. As part of the "wallpaper and border" bunch, she is out and about town, has it together, and is sharp. Admittedly, her volunteerism does service the community when it does not get in the way of her social life.

Both the "hard-edged volunteer/socialite" and the "simpleton" are seen as having time on their hands and able to pick up the slack for everyone— teachers, husbands, children, and neighbors. They both are seen as doing lots of driving. They have the luxury to raise their kids—taking them to the pumpkin patch in the fall, baking cookies in the winter, and lying around the pool with them on a lazy summer's day. She is commonly asked, "What do you do all day?"

MYTHS?

After reviewing these stereotypes, I have to answer the question, "Are these women real or fantasy?" And while you may recognize a *portion* of someone you know in these images, the women illustrated above are purely fictitious.

According to Laura Tracy, professor of women's studies at Georgetown University, in her book, *The Secret between Us: Competition among Women*, "We feel envious of the women with whom we compete. Envy indicates our desire for sameness, *not* for difference. . . . We experience envy when we meet someone who is different from us and, we think, better than we are. We covet what that person possesses because her possessions, whether material, physical, or intellectual, disconnect her from us."[1]

Extrapolating on Tracy's theory, women want the mother on the other side of the Wall to be either "dim-witted" or "the bad mother" to make them feel better about themselves. Hence, the callous stereotypes are created. So when women compare themselves to others, they are equating themselves to clichés and stereotypes, not the real world of others.

If these clichés aren't true, who are these women? What are their lives really like? Based on research, the next two chapters explore the lives of full-time employed and stay-at-home mothers, who they really are, and how they actually feel.

NOTE

1. Laura Tracy, *The Secret between Us: Competition among Women* (Boston: Little, Brown, 1991), p. 14.

FOUR

THE REALITY OF BEING A FULL-TIME EMPLOYED MOTHER

"Working is an integral part of me, like breathing; it's how I identify myself—it's my calling."

The reality of being a full-time career mother is not the stereotype, and unless another family member is the primary caretaker for their children, many employed mothers feel an abundance of guilt. After talking to over thirty mothers working full time outside of the home, I realize how difficult it is to balance aspirations for promotions, children's basketball games, birthday parties, business trips, dance recitals, major client presentations, and sick children. "Operating in survival mode" is how many of the mothers described their lives to me.

Most of these mothers discussed, totally unprompted, how they individually make time for their children, whether by walking with the youngest daughter, age four, by herself through the mall to get an ice cream cone so that she feels singled out and special or by playing a quick game of Horse on the basketball court with a ten-year-old son. Our challenge as mothers is to determine how to make a profession and motherhood succeed simultaneously.

PROS TO WORKING OUTSIDE THE HOME

Women with a vocation work for income, fulfillment, and self-esteem. While a few mothers work only to cover expenses and gain no pleasure from the experience, most women voice their enjoyment in getting out of the house and contributing to society. A paycheck is empowering; not having to ask your husband for money is empowering. Employed women savor having an identity beyond a mother, being independent by receiving compensation for their labors, and interacting with adults on a highly intellectual level. Our society respects a paycheck, labor that realizes compensation, and, therefore, the people who earn wages.

Income

"I equate dollars with independence, as I got to leave home and get away from my mother by earning my way out," says Amy, a marketing vice president. "Earning money is power. I need to earn money so that I can go where I want, eat the way I want, and dress the way I want. It's part of my self-definition. I personally need a paycheck because it gives me control of my life, helping me to define myself and my lifestyle."

Mothers relish financial freedom and making economic decisions in the household rather than having their husbands control the money. Hallie, a hair salon owner in Hartford, Connecticut, says that some of her at-home friends hide bundles of new children's clothes from their husbands because they are not earning money and feel guilty about the purchases. Yet she never conceals any of her purchases because she brings in a good portion of the total household income. Drawing a paycheck gives many of the women I interviewed permission to buy items that they may not otherwise acquire. They call it "shopping without guilt." Tammy, a real estate agent in Mount Kisco, New York, claims that she needs to earn some of the family income to order takeout for dinner without guilt, while Margaret, a Florida actuary, needs to earn a paycheck in order to spend money on herself. She will buy items for the children yet feels guilty about spending anything on herself unless she is bringing in income.

Many women interviewed not only earn a paycheck but also bring in the lion's share of the household income. Approximately a third of the employed mothers claim to be the major breadwinner of the family.

"I love what I do! I'm the higher paid of the two of us," expresses Sandra, owner of an advertising agency in Los Angeles. "This is the fourth year that I have owned the business, and I never tire of it. I love our lifestyle, too. My business generates over one million dollars annually, and we would have a huge lifestyle change if I stopped running my business."

Chris explains how she and her husband agreed on her income status. "While I bring in the greater percentage of the family income with my financial management job, I enjoy my position even more because my husband, Don, is happy. As a team, we decided that I would become the major breadwinner so that he could switch careers. Don was a high-flying, well-paid businessman who was discontented with his daily life. I supported him through additional schooling in order for him to gain his teaching certification so that he could instruct high school courses. Now he's a high school teacher and coach, experiencing fulfillment with his occupation. Don is *so* much happier, making our entire family situation more enjoyable. I've never looked back."

The other two-thirds of working-out-of-the-house women are broken equally into two groups, the first being focused on improving the family's quality of life. "We bought a new house so I had to go back to work"; "The kids are going to need the money in the future for their education"; "My salary is going into our retirement fund." These women are earning additional income to buy the bigger house or to fund the children's college education or to pay for a vacation that the family otherwise could not afford. The second group is employed to pay for the basics: food, rent, and clothing. Several mothers interviewed were holding down more than one job at a time. Gina was one of them. At one point, Gina was an assistant director of Mother's Day Out, sold jewelry, and baby-sat four children plus her own four in the house. While she holds down only one job as a paramedic today versus the three she held in the past, she still works to pay the rent and feed her children. In fact, she feels alienated from her sons and daughters because of her employment, but she has no choice in order to survive. She envies stay-at-home mothers and wishes she could be one of them.

And no wonder so many women must earn money. In the 1950s, a mortgage consumed about 14 percent of the average thirty-year-old's income, but, in 2001, approximately half of the money of medium- and low-income homeowners went toward housing. In addition, employee contributions toward healthcare costs rose 60 percent for a family of four between 1973 and 2000.[1]

But whether women worked for extra income to pay for a trip to Disney World or for covering the costs of feeding the family and a roof over their heads, most employed women believe it is good for the children to see that everyone has the ability to take care of themselves. Knowing that you can provide for yourself, especially as a woman, is an important lesson to teach children. Employed mothers feel that they teach by example, no matter why the money is being earned.

"You need to be able to take care of yourself, no matter what the situation. I started my own New Jersey business for extra spending money, and now I use it to feed my family. I formed my own partnership as an executive recruiter to meet my own needs," claims Jo Ellen. "It's important to show our children that everyone can work and support themselves."

As an added twist, several women whom I interviewed weren't employed for the actual dollars that they bring home weekly but for the healthcare benefits. Their husbands operate their own businesses, yielding poor healthcare benefits and, sometimes, none at all. Bringing home quality healthcare for their children is the goal for these mothers, certainly an admirable reason to work outside the home.

Identity

"I have chosen to continue to work even though I am juggling because I feel that if I quit, a part of me would be missing," claims Kelsey, a New Orleans teacher of disabled and handicapped children. "Each person in my family has something for themselves, so when we get together, we all get along well. My career actually enhances my family life."

Working provides not only income but also an adult identity beyond "mommy." Mothers relish the intellectual challenge brought on by employment. These women get a high from winning over Nike, Inc., as a new client; creating a new "look" in someone's living room through faux painting; developing a multimillion-dollar cost-savings program for Johnson & Johnson; watching several sick patients get well under their care; catering the perfect party; or creating Disney's advertising campaign for its latest movie. Setting goals and meeting objectives make these women feel productive, fulfilled, and energized. When some of them stayed home during maternity leave, they were "bored to tears" and "driven nuts" by their lack of productivity.

"I must feel productive. I trained and worked for a long time before having children, never thinking that I would stay home. Coming out of school, I had huge debt and had no option but to work. And now, even though I'm out of debt and have more choices, I still enjoy the pursuit of medicine and being a nurse practitioner," claims Doris from Kansas.

"It is part of my image of who I am. . . . That is why I work, not for the dollars. I'm happiest when I am moving forward and productive. Some women in my neighborhood resent that they have pushed their own life aside for their families and, therefore, also resent me and what I represent. My career gives me independence as I have my own income, my own money," reiterates marketing vice president Amy. "It isn't healthy for me to be at home. You need to take care of yourself emotionally and physically as a person so that you can be a good mother to your children."

The Reality of Being a Full-time Employed Mother

"I get my self-esteem from working," claims Anne, vice president of a promotion company. "When a presentation goes well, it feels really good. . . . My husband, Adam, never had that feeling; he never got that charge out of working that I got. When I was at H. J. Heinz, I was so excited about being there that I bought and wore a bright red suit. I just loved being part of the organization, I was so loyal!"

"My main job is education," claims Edith, a university medical professor. "I love to teach, having influence over the curriculum and using creativity. It's gratifying. I have often asked myself what I would do if I won the lottery. I would set up schools and do much of what I'm doing now but a little differently, more liberally, since money would not be an issue."

"When I was in my thirties, I regretted not living on my own before I got married. Then, when my husband started traveling a lot, I began gaining independence, learning who I was and how to be strong. Working was a big part of that," voices Phyllis, a church director.

In fact, because these mothers are energized and fulfilled by their work, they are better moms for it. Mothers themselves, as well as their friends, recognize how much better they relate to their children when they get a break from the kids during the day while pursuing interests that they enjoy.

"I'm passionate about work and never felt that it has taken away from me being a good mother." Ashley, who delivers long-term care for traumatic brain injury survivors in Charlotte, continues, "My work involves my kids and teaches them to be good people. They are sensitive and comfortable with people who have disabilities because of my professional pursuits. They would volunteer to help at the drop of a hat. Some days, I must admit, I work too many hours, but with my personality I would end up working all the time on volunteer work if I was not employed. I decided that I might as well get paid for doing the work. Not only do I have my job with forty-five to fifty hours per week, but I also have an additional ten hours with the case management company that I created. I saw a need in the community for one, and so I launched it. I am lucky that I have a supportive family so that I can do this."

"Everyone wants to do what is best for their kids, but being an at-home mother may not be what is best for you," states Lynn. "My best friend here in Portland can't stay home, saying that she would kill her children. . . . She is very open about it. She doesn't have a fabulous career. In fact, she can't even pay for the daycare with her salary."

"I had a friend who couldn't decide if she should go back to work or not—it was a moral issue for her." Helen continues, "The paycheck boosted her self-esteem as she now has two businesses and is her own person. The children are currently getting a nurturing mother versus the bitchy mom they were seeing in the past."

Annette, a physician, says, "My close friend has a PhD in English literature. She was dragged out of her second academic appointment so her husband could move to Idaho for his career, making her a miserable at-home mother. It took her a long time, but she eventually obtained a part-time high-powered professor's position. She's so much happier now."

And, not surprisingly, I spoke with a few women who have considered staying home with the children yet don't because they are afraid they will lose their identities, afraid they will not be able to reenter the workforce, afraid they will lean on their husbands too much, and afraid that they will be just plain bored.

According to Alison, a marketing consultant, "The challenge of the workplace, the variety of activities, and the money as well as keeping my brain awake, these are all the reasons that I work. Looking to the future, it's harder to get back in once you drop out. I saw my mother drop out. She owned a store and sold it when we were young and regretted it later. She had to start all over when we were in high school. That said, sometimes it's hard to stay in."

"Once your kids are older and you want to get back into work, what would you do? How would you get back in?" says Susan, an accountant.

CONS TO WORKING OUTSIDE THE HOME

When a mother is employed, she chooses to have power and control in the outside world—in hospitals, courts, corporations, and universities. Yet she hands many hours of her child's life over to the control of others, diminishing her time and influence as a primary caregiver.[2] Discussing this daily power-lessness over her children is difficult for an employed mother to do. It is easier to voice her longing for more time—more time for her children, more time for her husband, and more time for herself. And as wrong as it is, mothers who work outside the home are considered women who put themselves ahead of their children. Society tells Mom that employment should be for financial need only and that the mother at home is *the* gold standard. Such sacrifice of self is supposed to be the cornerstone of motherhood.[3] These societal attitudes add to the enormous guilt that employed women already feel regarding motherhood.

In addition to guilt and the lack of time, mothers easily describe the constant compromises being made between the family and the job. Janet, an employee relations manager for a large Detroit firm, speaks for most full-time employed mothers: "If I'm at home, I'm thinking about my e-mails at the office, and when I'm at the office, I'm thinking about Johnny's birthday party. I can't win."

No Time

"There's not enough time. . . . There's never any downtime. I'm keeping so many balls in the air: the house, the homework, the job, the children's activities. I am the crazy woman shopping at the grocery store at 10 p.m. I'm at the mall to buy birthday gifts right before it closes. And I never watch television. I fantasize about one week as a stay-at-home mom and what I would do," says Nancy, an attorney.

Nancy is not the only one who feels this way. Almost every mother with a full-time vocation interviewed voiced feelings of being harried, stressed, and under constant pressure from trying to manage for everyone in the family while also being employed. In fact, when employed mothers were asked what they liked least about their lives, almost every one said either the chaos and lack of downtime in her life or not having enough time with her children and husband. Most still do the laundry, the cleaning, the managing of the children's schedules, the grocery shopping, and the cooking themselves. They have *two* jobs instead of one.

Dr. Arlie Hochschild, a professor of sociology at Berkeley, states, "Most women who work at jobs during the day also work a 'second shift' at night, doing most of the shopping, cooking, housework, and, if there are children, parenting . . . putting in an extra month's work a year, in the form of chores at home. This double burden strains them to the limit."[4]

"As a mother with a profession, I do many things in one day," says Kentucky sales representative Andrea. "There isn't one moment that I'm not doing two things at a time. I make business phone calls and answer e-mails simultaneously: I slip a video into the VCR for my child while I am loading the washing machine; I am balancing my checkbook while talking to you during this interview; I vacuum and run the dishwasher while printing down orders from the computer. When I sit down, it is all over. I go to bed between 8:30 p.m. and 9 p.m. because I start working at 6:30 a.m."

"My sister asks why she should do two jobs when her husband does one, so she stays home. She bakes bread and pays half of what I spend at the grocery store because she cooks everything from scratch. She knits, she quilts, she is very inefficient, but then she can be—she has just one job. I must be super efficient because I have two jobs," claims graphic designer Debbie.

"When I lived in Kansas and my husband was working in another state, I had two kids at home with me. They had school; they had sports; they had homework, and I had a full-time job in human resources at a large manufacturing facility with no backup. I had to run a tight ship because every minute was accounted for. It was the worst time in my life because I never had any downtime," contends Elizabeth.

These moms have no hobbies; read few, if any, books; and watch little television because they have no time for themselves. Credit manager Sharon describes it well: "I wish I could stop the train and step off for one minute."

Chris says, "It is hard for me to relax because there is always something over my head that I didn't get a chance to do. I'm being pulled in forty directions."

And Tammy states, "The second shift starts when I get home."

"I give up sleep when I run out of time; I get up earlier," says Marcia. "I usually get up at 4:30 a.m. and can get up at 3:30 a.m. if necessary. Once, my family caught me running the washing machine at 4 a.m. I've learned to select quieter chores that early in the morning so as not to wake my family. I usually go to bed around 10:30 p.m. or so."

While carrying on business solely from home appears ideal, mothers who run their employment this way are generally dissatisfied. Since others know that she is home all day, they don't understand why she can't chat on the phone for thirty minutes or run out for a bite to eat at lunchtime. Separating business from the home is arduous since both activities are in the same location, particularly if the work space is located centrally within the home versus over a garage or in a basement, away from the main home activities.

"When you work from home, you never leave; there's always pressure, always something to be done. I'm either worrying about the bank statement or the business or the laundry," contends Calle, an office manager for an Internet company. "You can't work from home unless the kids are in school. I took one week maternity leave, that's it, five days. I never 'go home' from work—I'm always there. I never get that chance to walk in the door and take that breath when I come home, because I'm always there. I used to like relaxing when I came home, but I never do that now."

"Everyone thinks working from home is 'ideal,' but it is not because people think that I have lots of free time—even my husband wonders what I do all day. Where is the free time? I'm *working*," claims recruiter Jo Ellen. "Going to the office is much preferred, since everyone knows you should be focused there, but at home, people talk to you on the phone, forgetting that I'm 'at work' trying to get my projects completed by 5 p.m. If I had a separate phone line and office space in the basement, maybe I would like it more, but right now it's more difficult than leaving home."

And it comes as no surprise to see that these women have little time for friendships. "Full-time employed moms have no time for friends, as you must be committed to have a friendship with someone. You must make time for friends, and working mothers don't even have time for themselves." Laura, a hospital medical director, continues, "The kids are number one, work is number two, your relationship with your husband is number three, and you are number four. You never get to yourself, and you barely make it to your husband. You are last because you are a nurturing being and give in to everyone else first."

Yet these women want to maintain friendships with other women; they long to talk over a cup of coffee on a Saturday afternoon or a glass of wine on Friday night. But for numerous full-time working women, this is rarely possible.

"When I was working, to think of anything extra was beyond me. I was straining to keep my kids clean and put dinner on the table," says Diane, now an at-home mother in South Carolina. "Maybe that's what happens. Career mothers know that they just have time to wave to their neighbors and say 'hello,' nothing more. They will never get to follow up with a cup of coffee or with lunch on the patio because their life is so full already."

"We have a mothers' night out in my Pittsburgh neighborhood where women get together one night a month and play games. There is one professional mother in the neighborhood who comes when she can, but she feels like an outsider. She looks at the clock the whole time she's there," states at-home mom Molly.

"I currently have few friends because I just moved, and my church job takes all of my time," says Phyllis. "When I do have a little time, I take it

with my family. I would love to go out with other women for lunch or shopping, but the time isn't there. I really miss my friendships with women."

Guilt

"When I first went back to the office after having my first baby, I cried all the way to work. I was torn. Should I get a nanny? Should I use daycare? I wanted to be one of those mothers who could color all day with her kids, but I just couldn't do it—I don't have the patience. So instead, I have the guilt." claims Randi, a software documentation manager.

Guilt is defined as "feelings of culpability especially for imagined offenses or from a sense of inadequacy."[5] Since mothers are socialized to put everyone's needs before theirs, they feel these "imagined offenses" if they cannot attend a class play being held at 2 p.m. because of their office duties. Or Mom feels "a sense of inadequacy" when Suzy cries as she is being dropped off at the daycare center, even though Suzy toddles off to build a tower of blocks as soon as Mom is out of sight. Most women were initially silent about the guilt they feel, and some never mentioned it. Yet as the interviews progressed and the women became more open, the conversations eventually turned to guilt.

"Other professional moms make me feel as though I am more normal as we are going through the same things. I feel guilty and they feel guilty; we all are torn about giving enough to our children," declares Kathy, a vice president of operations. "I learned that everyone has to make their own conclusions based on needs—one decision is not the same for everyone. I initially felt as though I had made the wrong choice, but I eventually got over the guilt as a working mom."

"Ordinarily, it is a balancing act, but right now we are both working 24/7 for the next two months," says Barbara, a commodity trader. "I feel so guilty placing the kids in front of the TV as a surrogate baby-sitter, but there's nothing I can do about it. We're currently in survival mode."

A *Redbook* magazine survey affirms that guilt arises because working mothers believe that they shortchange their children by not being there to guide and protect them in a dangerous world.[6]

"The kids cry when you drop them off at daycare. . . . It pulls at your heartstrings. As my daughter got older, she would tell me that she missed me," says Jenny, a sales representative. "My kids missed me a lot because I had to work. I just hated that, but what could I do? I always thought that I would be a stay-at-home mom, but I work out of necessity."

Yet some mothers that I talked to had ways to help them overcome their guilt. Janet, an employee relations manager, was one of them. "When I was younger and even today, I feel I must make home-cooked meals and bake cookies. I feel that it's really important that we eat together. My sons tell me that I'm the only mom who makes cookies—everyone else gets theirs from Wal-Mart. I make lunch for my children every day, while most kids buy lunch. In fact, every Sunday afternoon I bake cookies or brownies for their lunches for the week as my ritual. As a career mom, this is important to me. Never being home with them, I feel it's important to eat as a family, so I make home-cooked dinners nightly. Most families are buying meals at Burger King, yet I'm getting us to sit down and eat together as a family whenever possible. A small part of me feels that I have missed something somewhere, but I can't imagine missing out on work."

"When my kids were younger and I had to work and didn't want to, it devastated me. I felt so guilty. But now, with many of my friends going to classes and working part-time because their children are going to school, I'm feeling so much better," claims Ashley.

For most women, employment is not a choice, and having their path chosen for them lessens the guilt. Knowing that the income is going toward the children's clothes, school supplies, and food relieves some of the guilt. In 1991, Jane Swigart revealed the same findings in her book, *The Myth of the Bad Mother: The Emotional Realities of Mothering*: "Some expressed relief that they had to work outside the home for economic reasons, because they felt society secretly condemns women for choosing to leave their children unless financially pressed."[7] Based on my conversations with women over the last year, I find that it is no different today.

"If money is the issue, it's easier to go back to work after having children. It alleviates the guilt and helps you with your path. I needed the money, so it guided my direction," divulges Judy, director of diversity. "My sister was divorced and had to work in an office to survive, so she had no guilt. Your path is determined by situations and guilt. You need something to push you in one direction or the other."

"When I stop work at night, I stop work. I don't continue to think about the progress of my projects or the ad campaign that is currently under development. My daughter, Susan, is my little friend. I had just one child at the age of thirty-nine. Part of me is still guilty though, and since I work virtually from home, sometimes I want to run out and go pick her up," declares Sandra, owner of her own advertising agency. "I try to balance work and family, but 9 a.m. to 5 p.m. is a long day at school for a four-year-old. If I quit for a few years, it would be devastating to me monetarily, as I would lose clients and have to start the business all over again from scratch."

Poor Treatment after Children

"I had no idea what the cost of pregnancy would be to my career, I was so naive," claims former Wall Street trader Elsie.

To top off the issues working-out-of-the-home mothers have, several women mentioned poor treatment by co-workers after giving birth, waiting for them to slip up or quit. Some mentioned that employers were pleased with them as long as the family was invisible to the office. One woman referred to a friend who had stellar reviews and exceeded expectations yet was told that she was out of the office too many days with sick children, and, therefore, she would not be promoted. Initially, I thought that sort of discrimination happened in the 1980s and early 1990s, but surely not now, not after the turn of the century. I was wrong. According to my data collected from the interviews, women are still incurring this poor treatment today. In fact, the Second US Court of Appeals said in the spring of 2004, "simply assuming that women with children would take their jobs less seriously than non-mothers was, in itself, discrimination."[8] This statement was made regarding a *current case* under appeal. "The Second Circuit held that an employment action based on stereotypes about motherhood is a form of gender discrimination."[9] The good news is that this ruling will make it easier for employed mothers to bring forth discrimination suits in the future.

Jo Ellen, currently an executive recruiter, tells her story of discrimination. "Four days after the twins were born, my boss needed to know if I was coming back. He said that he would create a special job for me with better hours for raising children if I was willing to give up a managerial job for a nonmanagerial job, as I was previously working from 7 a.m. to 7 p.m. I gave up the old position—which, by the way, was filled by two men—and started in the new one. Two weeks later, I was introduced to a new boss. He claimed that he did not need someone with shorter hours—either I worked from 7 a.m. to 7 p.m. or had no job at all. At this point, I was left with a nonmanagerial position as a trader with the same hours I had had with my position managing a currency trading desk. Everyone assumed that I was 'just a mother.' I wasn't given a chance.

"So I decided to leave," she continues. "When I handed in my resignation, my male boss said, 'I can't believe you are doing this to me.' He assumed that you couldn't run a desk if you were a mom. I wasn't willing to settle for a nonmanagement job working management hours. It was in the late 1980s, and mothers did not run trading desks. My boss *did* agree to severance pay. Before I received the severance check, I had to sign a document saying that I would not sue the company. They really wanted me to sign the papers and rushed me through them quickly. I briefly thought about suing, but dismissed it. If you get a reputation as a woman who sues, you won't get another job."

In the late 1980s, Felice N. Schwartz wrote a controversial article in the *Harvard Business Review* arguing that businesses needed to create policies to help mothers balance career and family responsibilities if they wanted to retain talented women in management. Detractors of the idea labeled the concept the "Mommy Track." Today, the "Mommy Track" holds a largely negative connotation, even though the base concept itself was meant to be positive. Schwartz's idea was to foster flexibility in the workplace for mothers. Yet this was lost because detractors focused on the idea that women have to choose between a family and a career, while fathers do not.[10]

Former banker Dawn reveals, "In my last review, where I had met all of my goals and all of my objectives, my boss used the words 'She is on the mommy track.' I asked him if he really wanted to use that wording in my review and let him think about it overnight. He rewrote my review the next day. I was so mad that the vein under my eye kept popping for two weeks afterwards. A year later, during my exit interview from the bank, the human resources people heard all of this and were shocked. They wanted to keep me, but it wasn't a hard decision to leave once I had made up my mind. They asked why I hadn't come to them when this happened. I thought that retelling this story would result in losing my job at the time, and, frankly, I needed the money."

Being treated poorly also includes being made unsure of your status as an employee. Here is the story of project engineer Irisa, who was yanked back and forth between full-time and part-time status unnecessarily. "When I first had my child, my boss kindly switched my hours to accommodate my baby. I had to catch the 4:35 p.m. train in order to get my child by 5:30 p.m., when the daycare was closing. So we agreed that I would work 9 a.m. to 4 p.m. straight through with no lunch. This enabled me to work my thirty-five hours per week as well as pick up my child on time. Unfortunately, that supervisor resigned eight months later. I then worked under a vice president who did not like my 9 a.m. to 4 p.m. arrangement, yet he did honor it. At the time my arrangement was made, the company considered part-time thirty-two and a half hours per week. Therefore, I was full time at my thirty-five hours per week obtaining full benefits.

"Soon thereafter, the head of human resources told me that by law I had to take a half-hour lunch. That put me at thirty-two and a half hours per week and placed me in the part-timer versus full-time category. This would cause a loss of benefits, which were very important to me as I was eight months pregnant at the time and needed the maternity benefits. The human resources director was clearly threatening to take away my paid maternity leave of absence. It was very odd that they brought up the issue when I was eight months pregnant and not earlier. Checking into the laws they were referring to, I determined that I was in the right and prepared to bring in a lawyer. But after discussing the situation with them, it wasn't necessary. So I had my daughter, receiving my short-term disability leave. When I came back to work, the vice president called me in and told me in order to remain employed, I would need to go to a sister company, which I did. There I received part-time status, losing all of my benefits. I did work through it though and now have a better supervisor, but it was situation made unusually difficult by the company."

Another woman, Colleen, a former loan officer from South Carolina, met with male attitude issues when she returned to the office after childbirth. "Working in a predominantly male department, I was the only woman in my section who came back to work after having a baby. The men had a betting pool as to what month I would quit after I had my daughter. I determined that I would remain at least six months so that no one would win the betting pool. I ended up staying twenty-four months."

Ann Crittenden, an award-winning economics journalist and author, agrees that children and careers are difficult to mix because of employers' attitudes. She has found that two children spaced closely together is incompatible with most women's careers, and that employers can be surprisingly unsupportive with notice of a second baby.[11] Crittenden backs up her statements with quotes from corporate experts such as Charles Rogers, a management consultant in Boston, who claims that time spent in the office matters as much as, if not more than, productivity in many corporations.[12]

And according to Joan C. Williams, American University's director of the program on work life law, childless women not in the office are assumed to be on business trips, but absent *mothers* are assumed to be grappling with daycare issues. In addition, full-time employed mothers are rated less businesslike and more like housewives. That is a significant disadvantage in a business environment because housewives are viewed on par with the elderly, blind, retarded, and disabled.[13] Mothers cannot get a break.

"My boss's outlook has changed since I've had children. Now he sees me as a 'mommy,' and it has hurt my career," declares Allie, a product manager. "When I told him that I was pregnant for the second time, he said 'My, my, look at your big family.' I told him that this was my last child, even though I didn't have to say anything."

Compromising Career or Family

"The most challenging part is succeeding in both motherhood and my career. Sometimes I must compromise one for a while and then switch, compromising in the other. Some weekends I must spend time on work writing, preparing, and practicing big presentations," admits Ronnie, a director of procurement in large corporation. "I make it up to the family in other ways— the quality of time spent with the children is what is important. I could say that I have reached a point where I want to back off on my career, but that's not true. The hard part is staying in tune with my children while I move upward. . . . I must stay in tune with my children. I want to be home for those big events for my children such as their birthdays, Valentine's Day, and Halloween. This may limit my movement to the next level in my career, forcing me to make hard choices over the next several years."

Bridget, an attorney at a Fortune 100 corporation, agrees with Ronnie regarding the time spent to snare the top jobs. "I haven't identified with high-powered career moms as it's important for me to be involved in school and my daughters' Girl Scout troops. I don't want the next position up the ladder right now because that would be a vice-presidential-level job involving lots of travel. Right now, I have flexibility, I can take a half day or get away when necessary to see the kids in school. I control my work. I know professional mothers going to Mexico, while their husbands also have high-level corporate positions. I don't know how they do it. I have found a good balance, but my career isn't as fast as it could have been."

She is just one example of the many women who have redefined success for themselves to accommodate their families. These women are not taking the fastest way to the top because that could jeopardize their relationships with their children and husbands. This was a theme with several mothers who stated that the higher level the job, the longer the hours. Hence, it is more difficult to have a successful, top-level career while juggling motherhood. Gratifying, intriguing work, along with the appropriate salary, keeps them happy while the children are younger. Yet when the children are older and they are ready to push full force again, they can rarely do so within the same company. They will always be seen as a "mommy" first and a career women second for the uppermost jobs.

"In a big corporation, if you decide to stay home and then come back later, you've taken your piece off the chessboard. A two-year leave of absence takes you out of play among the front-running candidates," claims Ronnie. "You can be a middle candidate, but you're no longer at the top of the list."

Jenny, a sales representative at a large corporation in Illinois, agrees. "You may be perceived as less serious and put on a slower track if you utilize corporate family-friendly policies such as flextime. Yes, the policies are there, but if you use them, everyone in the office starts wondering about your loyalty and commitment to the job, wondering if you're able to handle emergencies if they interfere with your set hours. When promotions come up, you will *not* be at the top of the list as you aren't seen as giving 110 percent."

As a way to succeed at one's own pace, Bridget feels mothers should work in one place while they are pregnant and their children are small because that is when they are identified as "mothers." Once they want to push ahead in their careers, they should change companies. Then, the new corporation will not see them as "mothers" because their outlook and lifestyle have changed. While Bridget hasn't done this herself yet, she believes it is the best way for mothers to maximize their careers. I found it an interesting concept as it allows mothers flexibility when they need it and advancement when they want it.

After having children, some mothers found themselves not giving 100 percent as they had in the past, signified by such actions as changing meeting times to accommodate children, so that they could ensure daycare coverage.

The Reality of Being a Full-time Employed Mother

"We had a huge snowstorm one day in February, and the nanny couldn't get to the house. Unfortunately, I had a 9 a.m. meeting with the chairman of the company that day. I had to bring my son to work with me, a one-year-old! I had no options," declares Hope, director of corporate relations at a multi-billion-dollar firm. "After that, I started compromising my work by setting up meetings at 10 a.m. or later. I taught corporate classes and would have twenty people who had flown in from all over the United States for a training session waiting for me in a classroom. I had no backup if I didn't show up. I needed to begin classes later to give me time to find help with my son in case of difficulties. I felt as though I wasn't giving the job 100 percent, what I had always given it in the past, but I had no choice."

Other mothers found themselves actually lowering their career aspirations and not pushing themselves toward the next position so that they could have more time with their children. These women, uncomfortable with not pushing their careers forward, were torn over the best solution.

"What really hurts is you want to go back, carry your own weight, yet you impose limitations on yourself," reveals Joy. "When I went back to work, I said to myself that I wouldn't travel and commute a long way for the sake of my family. So I had to reenter the workforce after taking time off at a lower-level position than my previous job. It's hard on my ego as I miss the suit, the briefcase, and the airline travel. Even though I built the hurdle myself, I still want it all. I know that I have to pick and choose, but I'm human. . . . It eats away at your professional side—it's a compromise."

Sheila retells a story regarding her best friend's experience with motherhood versus careers. "Shannon had a good job but was not putting her whole self behind the career. When her co-worker and good friend Jessica came back to work after maternity leave and put 110 percent behind her career, she received promotions and started shooting up the corporate ladder. Shannon thought of putting more of herself into her job to get promoted as well, meaning lots of travel and missing her kids quite a bit. She was torn over what to do by getting caught up in the corporate promotion cycle. It all comes down to time, a choice of family or career. You must do what is right for you."

Sandra realized that she could not manage two or more children and her advertising agency simultaneously, resulting in her being the mother of one. Yet now she feels she has compromised her family for her profession. "I only had one child on purpose because of the career trade-offs. The job was too big to have more than one child and continue working full time. Extra children would just be too much; I would have needed so much more help with childcare. Yet only having one child is my biggest regret."

According to a controversial article in the *New York Times Magazine*, "the talk of this new decade is less about the obstacles faced by women than it is about the obstacles faced by mothers."[14] In that article, Joan C. Williams is quoted as saying, "Many women never get 'near' that glass ceiling, because 'they are stopped long before by the maternal wall.'"

Women such as Audrey already know that. "Systematically there are problems with both sides. Few women pursue the big careers because it means not seeing their children. Those who are employed full time require flexibility on snow days, when the children are out of school, or days when the kids are sick are reticent to demand equal pay. They can't afford to get fired."

WHAT MAKES IT WORK

With all the downsides to mixing employment with motherhood, one might draw the conclusion that mothers with full-time occupations are a disgruntled group. Yet the majority of them are not. Why? What makes it work for them? Cheerful, satisfied, full-time employed mothers have great support and good daycare and have found ways to balance their lives. They are a creative and flexible group who can react well to whatever is thrown at them because of the support systems that they have built around themselves.

Support

"My sister's mother-in-law cleans her house, picks up the children from school, gets them started on homework, and starts cooking dinner. Having that kind of support makes a *big* difference," says Southerner Carly. "There're many working moms who have parents young enough to be able to drive their children around and help in emergencies giving lots of support. That's how they, like my sister, can do it all—with an abundance of support."

Maintaining a solid support network is crucial to employed mothers. This network can comprise husbands, friends, relatives, paid sitters, daycare centers, employers, or a mixture of them all. Going far beyond simple daycare, a support system can be used at any time of day or night for emergencies such as sickness or overnight childcare coverage for unplanned business trips. A complete system also entails help with the day-to-day details of cleaning and cooking and provides daily emotional backing. Some mothers affirm that their parents labor as much for their families as they do themselves. Their comments regarding the grandparents are "constantly having us over for dinner," "stopping by and folding laundry," and "coming over to watch the kids when they are sick." Others who have no immediate family in the area contend that if it were not for helpful neighbors, they could not make it through the week.

"Traveling around the world, attending late-night meetings, preparing presentations after dinner—that is the life of a top executive. My neighbor is one of those executives, a vice president at a major corporation, and a mother as well. She has her mother take care of the children, while her husband is the primary parent. He has the secondary job in the family as a cab driver in Chicago. Because her mother lives with the family, she has no privacy at all, yet she does have a solid support system. She attends many of the children's soccer and basketball games. She's clearly doing her best to balance her family life with her professional one, probably better than any father would in the same position," contends Jenny.

"When I first had my daughter, I worked every minute, maintaining four part-time jobs in Cleveland, using my parents as sitters," conveys Ruth. "In the mornings during the week, I attended one or two classes a semester. From there, I guided tours from 10 a.m. to 4 p.m. Then, at home in the evenings, I transcribed professors' lectures and typed them. Again on Saturdays, I guided tours from 10 a.m. to 4 p.m., then acted as a waitress for a caterer at night. And on Sundays, I cleaned homes for friends, studying whenever I could fit it in. During those first few years, I didn't sleep much—it was just insane, and I can't imagine keeping those hours now. God gives us strength when we need it. My parents helped me by cooking, doing the laundry, and running errands, making it possible for me to keep all the balls in the air without dropping one. Now I have just one steady job as a secretary and occasionally waitress weddings on the side."

Calle's support comes—surprisingly—from her supervisor. "I work from home because my husband is in the military, and, therefore, we move about every two years or so. My job is being the office manager for an Internet company and moves easily with me. If I didn't have this job, I would have to take a military job where I was overqualified and underpaid versus what I have the ability to do. I have a very understanding boss who works to support me, making this all possible."

And enough can't be said for supportive husbands. Eighty percent of the employed mothers raved about their husbands, claiming that if not for their spouse's help, an occupation would be impossible.

"My husband is very helpful: he does the laundry, loads and unloads the dishwasher, and ensures that homework is done," boasts Tammy. "He spends all of Saturday together with my son, Kurt, running from sports activity to sports activity. I run to the club to exercise and then hit the grocery store. The whole family knows the Saturday drill. In the summer, we also try to hit the pool in the afternoon, while Saturday night is for the adults. On Saturday evenings, Kurt has a different sitter than the rest of the week. He has his own thing going with his Saturday sitter and looks forward to her coming over. The success of my house is everyone participating in activities they really enjoy and my husband fully supporting it."

As a sales representative, Andrea is traveling quite a bit and needs her husband's assistance in order to maintain her sanity. In fact, without her husband's support, she wouldn't be holding her current, lucrative position. "I am always gone. My husband and I both work forty-five minutes from home and in opposite directions. At one point, when I was looking to switch jobs so that we would be working in the same city, my husband realized how desperate I was and set up an office in our hometown. As an accountant, he has freedom that I don't. He now works two days per week in our hometown to relieve me from the 'after-school pressure.' He's done on those days at 3:15 p.m., so he can pick up the kids from school and then continue his work from home."

Another mother, software executive Shami, related how she, much like Andrea, couldn't have continued on her career path without her husband's help. "While I was commuting every week between Kansas and California, I had a nanny who came and went during the day. I was gone Monday through Friday, forcing my husband to be home at 6:30 every night. He made dinner for the kids and did the laundry during the week as he was basically a single parent Monday through Friday with four children. On weekends we both cleaned the house, shopped for groceries, paid the bills, and the kids went with us wherever we went. Neither one of us ever rested or blinked an eye or even thought about it."

And Jamie tells how her husband was her partner in caring for ill children. "If my son, John, was sick, I would work in the morning, and my husband would work in the afternoon, each one taking turns so neither one would fall behind. If one had an engagement that demanded a full day's work, that person would go in all day and then stay home the next day if John was still ill. My son appreciates getting attention from both parents when he needs it."

Support from their spouses isn't only about childcare but also about "mothercare." Andrea says, "My husband and I send each other cards to the office when we feel the need, if something has gone wrong, if an emergency is over, or if we have not had a chance to speak to one another for a week. It is a good way to let the other one know that we still love each other."

Randi agrees. "My husband grounds me. He says, 'Your body is here, but your mind is not. Go finish your work and come back with all of you.'"

"I've survived three corporate downsizings and when my world changes at work, I wonder, where are my roots? Where is my support system?" says Anne, vice president of a promotions company. "It always leads me back home to my husband, Adam, and son, Zach. Adam, Zach, and I are a team against the world."

Another integral part of the support network is friends with common interests and values, particularly for those employed mothers who don't have relatives living in proximity. While getting together with friends is limited because of the many obligations, mothers "talk" through e-mail because it is not intrusive and can be written at 6 a.m. or midnight, bolstering each other's confidence in their management of the children. When they have phone conversations, it is usually in five- or six-minute intervals between greeting clients, attending meetings, servicing customers, or carpooling the kids. Occasionally, they meet at lunch during the week and see each on weekends when possible. In addition to emotional support, friends are an intricate, essential piece in the physical daily schedule for many employed moms.

"My neighbor and I trade off who will get the children after work. We check with each other during the day to see who has the most flexibility or who is having a bad day. It's been a lifesaver for both of us," explains physician Annette.

"I have more in common with full-time employed moms because I can talk to them about my two girls without guilt," says vice president of operations Kathy. "I can't relate like this with the men in my office or with at-home mothers because I need to share nanny issues with my friends. We bounce frustrations off of each other and connect mind-to-mind during trips together and occasionally at lunch, but we never hang out after work because we all live too far away from one another. These women are my support system."

Jillian, a respiratory therapist, adds, "We interact with other couples whose children are the same age as ours. The kids play outside, while we barbeque, hang out, and drink wine on weekends. Generally, we watch the kids swimming in the pool on Saturdays, staying in the neighborhood and not going anywhere else. We are socializing with our friends while still interacting with the kids, making it guiltfree."

"Finding time for friends is difficult. We had a play group with six families every Friday night for one and a half years. The whole family went, everyone: kids, moms, and dads. Now we only have a chance to meet once a month, but it is so great when we do!" explains Debbie.

Daycare

Childcare is the single part of the support network that must always be in place and *can't* break down. Since daycare *is* the focal point of the Wall, I have added a subsequent chapter focusing on childcare alone and so will briefly mention it here. It is the single largest factor in determining whether women continue to stay with an occupation or remain at home. Ranging anywhere from individual, in-home arrangements to full-day childcare centers; from grandma picking up the boys after school to a daycare facility handling after-school activities; from mom using a nanny in-home from 9 a.m. to 1 p.m. while she works in the study; to the girls being dropped off at Mother's Day Out two mornings a week so mom can call on clients in person, each daycare arrangement is designed to meet the financial, physical, and emotional needs of individual families.

Alison, a marketing consultant, has used a mix of in-home childcare to meet her needs: "We loved the first childcare giver my children had. She was an elderly woman who watched my kids in her own home for several years when they were young, but then I moved and started with the nannies. The first nanny I hired came from 7 a.m. to 6:30 p.m. Monday through Friday and lasted for two years. Once she left, however, I rolled four nannies in a row quickly. I was lucky with the first nanny, but not as fortunate after that.

"One nanny of mine was Elizabeth from Germany," Alison continues. "She was twenty-six years old and seemed a bit overwhelmed taking care of two young children, a sixteen-month-old and a three-year-old, but she did not complain. One evening after a busy day, she told me in a jittery voice that her father had had a heart attack and that she needed to fly to Germany right away. Totally understanding the situation, my husband and I not only arranged her flight for the next day but also paid for her ticket. After a week went by and we had not heard from her, I called her home in Germany out of concern for Elizabeth as well as her father. Her mother claimed that her father was fine but that Elizabeth was unavailable. Elizabeth never returned the first call and when I phoned a second time, her mother stated that Elizabeth was in the US and gave me no more information than that. I called her apartment leaving messages, phoned her boyfriend asking Elizabeth's whereabouts, but never heard from her again.

"The next nanny, Mary, had a husband who owned a restaurant. Unbeknown to me, she was staying up until 3 a.m. helping her husband close the restaurant, then coming to my house at 7 a.m. At the time, I had three children in school and one age two, who did not talk yet, at home. One morning when I had worked from home, I left for a meeting around 9:30 or so. As I was on my way to the office, I realized that I had left an important document on my desk at home, so I turned the car around to retrieve it.

"Upon reaching home, I passed the guest bedroom on my way to the study. Glancing in, I saw a line of children's books at the bottom of the bed. My daughter saw me and came running over to greet me. As I picked her up and hugged her, I strolled into the room. Fully expecting the nanny to be sitting on the other end of the bed, I was shocked to see her lying down under the covers, snoring. When I went to wake her, I called her name, 'Mary,' and she did not respond. Then I said her name louder, 'Mary,' and she still did not respond. Finally, I had to shake her really hard to arouse her. Obviously, I fired her on the spot. In hindsight, I feel that I should have seen it coming, as there had been little clues. Dropping in unexpectedly, I had seen my daughter coloring on the porch with Mary nodding off. Yet I was still surprised when it happened. If I had a nanny now with young children, I would have a NannyCam for sure."

Alison treated the nannies well, the same way she would like to be treated as an employee. "I tried to get to know them, always stocked the refrigerator with their favorite food and drinks, giving them gift baskets on their first day of work. After several weeks on the job, we sat down together and had honest discussions on what we could do to improve any issues that either of us saw arising. Yet most of the nannies that I hired didn't have a big work ethic—they did not treat the work as a job. In four and a half years, I rolled through six nannies."

But the majority of mothers can't afford nannies and put together a patchwork of help throughout their children's lives to accommodate their needs. Kelsey delineates her daycare situation. "My sons, Peter and Grant, have a sitter in my home on Monday and Wednesday afternoons, go to an after-school program on Tuesdays, and my parents watch them at their home on Thursdays and Fridays. This piecemealed arrangement works well for me as long as Peter and Grant are not sick and it doesn't snow. Those two things can cause havoc in my life. As an additional bonus, my parents have all of us over for dinner on Friday night, the one night of the week when I relish having someone else cook for me the most."

As a social worker, Mary Anne was paranoid about daycare and did lots of research before deciding where to place her children. I selected a daycare facility with a school-like atmosphere for my two daughters. Placing our children in a facility where parents could drop in regularly as well as one that was also regulated and accredited was important to me. Both my husband and I adjusted our work schedules to accommodate the childcare hours. While it was costly, especially for two children, I felt it was worth the price for my peace of mind."

Allie, on the other hand, selected in-home childcare providers over a daycare center when her son was a baby and a toddler. "The company paid an agency that recommended sitters and daycare, but it was up to the parents to explore the options. I never found any type of daycare down that path. The options were always unacceptable. I actually ran ads in the newspaper to find my best daycare providers. One in particular was great and watched my children in her own home. Since she loved babies, I took a newborn to her. She cuddled with my son, sang to him, read to him, and held him a lot. Her only problem was that she couldn't say no, resulting in taking care of too many kids at the same time. Despite that, we had an excellent working relationship with her. But by the time he was two years old, he needed to be moved where there were more toddlers like him.

"Luckily, the next daycare provider I found also had a son close to my son's age and in her own home," Allie continues. "She had a degree in chemistry, was into safety, and enjoyed teaching the children. She taught the boys lessons and took them to the local park for town-sponsored activities that I never could have taken my son to because of my working hours. She was more rigid and ran the daycare like a business. If you were late on picking your child up, you paid extra. We signed a contract with her when we started, agreeing to the business aspect of the childcare. She was much less flexible than the others that we had interviewed, making it very stressful for my husband and myself. Once I had to pay $130 extra for being late by twenty minutes."

She adds, "The worst daycare situation that we experienced was actually in the nicest home environment and best physical setup for children. Initially, she would call me at work at 5 p.m. once in a great while and say that she had to get to the bank prior to its closing—would it be okay if her teenager watched my son until 5:30 p.m. when I was scheduled to pick him up. I had met all of her children and felt that they were reliable and said that it would be fine. But when we began to hear about her upcoming divorce, we noticed that she appeared flaky and unreliable. This seemed to get worse as time went on. At times, she wasn't there when we would pick up our son. We had received no phone calls asking if this was all right or not, and while her teenagers covered for her, they offered no explanations. This went on for about three weeks before we removed our son from her care. I felt extreme anxiety the whole time this was happening. The level of supervision was deteriorating before our eyes, making me feel like the worst parent and more and more guilty day by day.

"Then, we used my mother-in-law for a babysitter for about a year and a half. She needed income, and we needed a sitter. What a match! We paid her, yet it took a toll on her health as well as an emotional toll on our son since she could not stimulate him mentally or physically the way he needed it.

"It was a patchwork of putting together care with people that I trusted. Needing to leave work when I wasn't ready as well as the challenge of finding quality daycare were the two hardest tasks for me. I would never want to go through that again. Now he has extended care at school."

Judy, director of diversity, articulates it well. "There was an article in the *New York Times Magazine* regarding opting out that really annoyed me. It talked about women making hundreds of thousands of dollars and having nannies, making the assumption that most women have nannies to complete all their dirty work. This isn't the reality for a majority of the women out there as most working moms don't have that, have no one to run the errands, wash the kids' clothes, or feed the children three times a day other than themselves. I call this assumptive nanny situation the 'white women of privileges perspective.' Most of us simply don't have the choice to be employed or not to be employed, to have nannies or not to have nannies."

Striking a Balance

"When I was employed full time, some women said that I was going to miss the first steps of my children, their first words, but I was looking at my next promotion. The first words that I heard them speak were their first words to me. I went to the office and when I was getting frustrated with my job, then I would go home. When the family began to drain me, then I would go back to work, creating the perfect balance for me. I would have longed for the one that I was missing if I hadn't done both," says lawyer Bridget.

Striking a balance between job and family makes employed mothers happiest. Some women find this balance by simply having both worlds available to them daily, while others maximize their family life by restricting hours given to those outside the household. Socializing after work with peers is not an option for most employed mothers because they are hurrying home to cook dinner or take children to sports activities. And for some, even socializing on the weekends includes the whole family.

"To strike a balance, I have no best friend other than my husband. I have no women friends as I have no time between husband, children, and employment for a friend. If I have two or three hours to give, I give it to the children. I try to do an activity with each one of them singly whenever possible so they each feel individually loved," claims Sophia, a factory worker. "The only time my husband and I are alone together is when we go to the grocery store. We go out on Saturday night to grocery shop and get a quiet cup of coffee together. It's our time with one another. Sunday is spent supporting my church and teaching Sunday school."

Janet, however, attacks the issues differently. "I make an effort to have play dates on Saturday and Sunday for my son while my husband and I socialize with the parents. We are energized as a mother and father when we interact with other working parents on weekends this way. By reinforcing our parenting style in this manner, we create a positive family atmosphere. And when you are a working-out-of-the-house mother, you have the benefit of never getting tired of your children. I am never annoyed or frustrated by my son as some of my stay-at-home relatives are with their children."

For some women, balance has never been a major issue because they have organized either their lives or employment in a way that works well for them. Several women interviewed are rising in their careers as their children grow. Building up to the "big jobs" as their children mature is a workable situation for them. The long, extended hours of top executives are in front of them, allowing them to be home at a reasonable hour when their children are young.

"I had my son and daughter early in my career, so I have older children as an executive. Caretaking is different when the kids are older—it isn't physical. I had not developed an executive identity yet when I started a family, so my identity evolved as the children grew. I balanced the family all along as I rose up through the ranks," declares Melissa, a vice president of business development with a large corporation. "Once you are an executive, you can't go backwards. To me, it's much harder to be an executive first and have the children second."

For others like Sandra, a successful strategy is limiting the number of children that they have. "My husband is gone four days per week, and I work full time five days a week, so we must be fair to my daughter and not have another child until one of us changes jobs. I don't want to look back and say, 'Why did I do that? Why did I have two children when I can't give either one of them enough time or attention?'"

A fortunate few are able to adjust their hours to meet their family's needs. Nicki comments on her flexible schedule: "I've been lucky. I have always either worked for supportive employers or myself. As a mother, I have never had to choose. Since I developed and ran my own market research company, I could work from home, calling my own hours and utilizing a sitter in crunch periods. Once I sold the company, I still determined my own hours, but held a more traditional office routine as my sons were in middle school by then."

HOW THE REAL FULL-TIME EMPLOYED MOTHER SUCCEEDS

Unlike the stereotype people have of full-time working mothers, every mother I interviewed truly cares for her children and is constantly concerned about their well-being. Helen's statement is typical for employed mothers: "As the girls age, the juggling becomes more and more challenging. Their needs are different. They will clam up if no one is there to talk to, so I need that open line of communication; I must be available; I must start the conversation. If you aren't there, you aren't there—there's no substitute for physical presence. I try to work my hours around my children as best I can.

The hardest thing with kids is to strike a balance between family quality time and work. I try to be on top of my game in both places."

Since her children's birth, Chris had been a full-time employed mother. She has a loving husband and two scholarly teenage girls who are active in athletics and the Girl Scouts. In fact, Chris is the leader for both troops! How does she do it? Chris replies, "You mean, you want my recipe for success?" That is exactly what I was looking for—and she had quite a bit to say.

Chris claims that it is not one or two tricks that make it come together, but an interconnected host of items, each one reinforcing and strengthening the other. Her first comments relate to the number of children and her husband. She has two children, one per parent, as both parents help out with tasks relating to the girls. Her sense is that more children might have been too much for her considering her occupational position, but two is perfect. Having her husband, Don, always available is also a major help. His full-time job requires no travel, so Chris can always count on him to be there when she needs it. He cooks dinner, she does the laundry. He drives one way with the first daughter, she drives the other way with the second. They split the chores so no one shoulders an inordinate amount of labor or carpooling. Since both are employed, they understand how tired the other one might be at the end of an evening.

She admits to making a few of those necessary phone calls and pulling together personal priority lists for organizational purposes at the office about an hour a day. Running errands at lunch and constantly checking her lists keeps her on top of things. While she does run *two* Girl Scout troops as a method to maintain constant interaction with her children, she does *not* volunteer at the schools at all. Chris knows that she can't do everything and remain employed full time, so volunteering at school doesn't make her priority list.

Never moving was another form of assistance. Since Chris has been in the same town from the time her children were in kindergarten, she has a network of other mothers for carpooling to sports, clubs, and religious activities. This also means that her children have a tight-knit group of friends whom she knows well and trusts. She states that she is fortunate that her girls are not needy or dependent on her, possibly due to their consistent environment and long-term friendships with schoolmates. Recognizing all the names of the children and parents at get-togethers ensures Chris that her children are in good company. In addition to never moving from one town, she has never changed companies either. Retaining positions within the same corporation has given her the ability to take off time for family obligations whenever necessary. Chris's superiors at the office know her and her working abilities so well that they assume that she will complete her projects on a timely basis, time off or not. Chris divulges that this was an earned privilege, not a given right by her company.

Last, unlike many full-time employed mothers, Chris actually has time to meet with girlfriends once or twice a month on a Friday night. All of the intertwined elements listed above, not just one or two of them, make that possible, and Chris believes that if one fell away, her well-tuned world would crumble quickly and be in need of repair. She is a great example of how it can be done.

Being selective in volunteer work, having a spouse who splits the chores and errands, remaining employed with one organization over a long timeframe, not moving from town to town or state to state, using lunchtime efficiently, and limiting the size of their families was mentioned to me not only by Chris but also by several other career women as the formula for their success.

Faye, a senior vice president and underwriting insurance manager, brought up many of the same points as Chris. Over fourteen years, she has worked toward gaining the trust and confidence that must be earned with senior management and her colleagues. She has proved herself to her employer and has been in her high position long enough so that she can take a morning to volunteer for her daughters and then work from home. Faye feels, however, that she has made concessions on how fast she has moved her career forward by leaving at 5:30 p.m. each evening as she refuses to give up her early evenings with her daughters.

Her husband, another major factor in her success, not only runs errands but also takes her career seriously. "I've never had to have *that* discussion," Faye claims. "Constantly prioritizing the schedules makes our routine run smoothly as possible. We have ten-minute meetings each night reviewing the next day, deciding who has what, looking at what must get done, and breaking up the list between us. Even the girls are included. When we have evening activities the next day, we discuss if dinner will be before or after the event so we know what type of snack the girls should have after school, large or small. Communication, coordination, and flexibility are key. When we see a list of ten items to do, we select the most important five and complete those. You can only do what is most urgent or significant to you."

"My girls missed out on play dates when they were small and in daycare. That was the hardest part. We did a lot of winging it when they were young. But now that they are in elementary and middle school, we coach softball for their teams at night in the spring and have sleepovers on weekends. Family time is still tight, but the girls have adapted well to our flexible schedules and roll with it. I am understanding, appreciative, and cognizant of what makes a family run well. Just order pizza when in a crunch and have everyone help out with the laundry. There is little 'invisible woman's work' as my husband helps out with the chores.

"It takes good planning and excellent organizational skills to stay on top of everything," adds Faye. "Having a structured schedule gives us the ability to do more than if we did not have one. All our doctors' appointments are made far in advance as either the first or last appointments of the day, evening appointments if possible. It is as though I am always ahead of myself. And while I currently have little time for myself, I am fortunate that I have full support from all my relatives as I get no heat for working full time from anyone. In fact, my parents are young enough to help baby-sit for the girls when we both have to travel at the same time or if we want to take a couple of days alone for ourselves."

Based on these perspectives along with others, the majority of full-time employed women with children are constantly balancing between the family and their vocation, focusing on those tasks that are most important at the time and letting the rest go. They may not have the cleanest house on the block or cook homemade dinners nightly or sew the Halloween costumes by hand, *but* they spend what time they have available at home on their children and husbands, weaving the bonds that form a family.

NOTES

1. Judith Warner, *Perfect Madness: Motherhood in the Age of Anxiety* (New York: Riverhead Books, 2005), p. 202.

2. Jane Swigart, *The Myth of the Bad Mother: The Emotional Realities of Mothering* (New York: Doubleday, 1991), p. 95.

3. Ibid.

4. Shirley Sloan Fader, *Wait a Minute, You Can Have It All: How Working Wives Can Stop Feeling Overwhelmed and Start Enjoying Life* (New York: G. P. Putman's Sons, 1993), pp. 16–17.

5. Henry Bosley Woolf, editor in chief, *Webster's New Collegiate Dictionary* (Springfield, MA: G. & C. Merriam, 1974), p. 510.

6. Pamela Paul, "What Moms Want Now; Second-Guessing Your Choice about Whether to Work or Not? Join the Club: Our Groundbreaking Survey Reveals a Fascinating New Shift in What Mothers Today Are Really Yearning for," *Redbook* (March 2003): http://www.web7.infotrac.galegroup.com/itw/infomark/591/883/52465874w7/purl=rcl_GRGM... (accessed October 15, 2004).

7. Swigart, *The Myth of the Bad Mother*, p. 32.

8. Jon Vuocolo, "Working Moms Catch Break in Court," *Wall Street Journal* (April 28, 2004): D3.

9. Ibid.

10. Linda Aburdene and John Naisbitt, *Megatrends for Women* (New York: Villard Books, 1992) p. 99.

11. Ann Crittenden, *The Price of Motherhood: Why the Most Important Job in the World Is Still the Least Valued* (New York: Henry Holt, 2001), p. 102.

12. Ibid., p. 99.

13. Joan C. Williams, "The Maternal Wall," *Harvard Business Review* (October 2004): 26.

14. Lisa Belkin, "The Opt Out Revolution," *New York Times*, October 26, 2003, http://www.nytimes.com/2003/10/26/magazine/26/WOMEN.html (accessed October 27, 2003).

FIVE

THE REALITY OF BEING A STAY-AT-HOME MOTHER

"Motherhood is the hardest, lowest-paying, most rewarding job of all."

Either she is so "simple" that she is incapable of being employed, or she is such an aggressive socialite and volunteer that she has a staff completing her household chores—these are the myths surrounding the at-home mom. The factuality of her life is that she has chosen to leave the workplace to improve the quality of her family life and make time for herself as well. Sacrificing her career, at least for the meantime, is a calculated decision. She has had the "rush, rush" life of full-time employment and enjoys a slower pace. While her at-home life is by no means perfect, she has little identity, and her professional neighbors envision her as dull and maybe even stupid, she prefers it over a stress-filled employed life. Although she is underappreciated by many because of her lack of income, her fulfillment is generated through a happy, lower-pressure family environment and self-directed projects.

PROS TO BEING A STAY-AT-HOME MOM

Every stay-at-home mother whom I interviewed worked prior to being home with her children. These were successfully employed women—bankers, real estate agents, doctors, engineers, teachers, graphic designers, secretaries, accountants, lawyers, sales representatives, dietitians, computer network designers, brand managers, and travel agents, to name some of them. While numerous employed mothers, and even some of the stay-at-home moms themselves, assert that at-home moms are dull and without the brainpower to maintain a job, I didn't find that to be the case. The mothers I talked to were *not* incompetent, were *not* passive, and certainly were *not* content to sit around and watch television all day. They made a conscious decision to leave the workplace in order to improve their family situation, enjoy more time with their children and husbands, run a smoother household, ensure discipline in the household, and have time for themselves.

Quality of Family Life

"I've made the right choice for me. . . . Women who earn money for a high lifestyle are sending the signal to their children that they are not important . . . that money is important and being busy is important, not that downtime with Mom and Dad is important," says Melinda, Asheville stay-at-home mother. "Now I would almost go into debt to stay at home with my children and keep my home running smoothly."

Three-quarters of the interviewed stay-at-home mothers left the workplace because they did not like the family trade-offs that they were making while being employed and raising children. For some women, the compromises were daycare issues—nineteen-year-old nannies from Idaho wanting to see New York City, using baby-sitting as a ticket to fulfill their dreams, or childcare providers using the television as a pacifier at daycare centers—while for others it was a need to get better connected with their children. Yet for many, the trade-off was purely about chaos in the household and juggling ten balls in the air at once.

Quality Time

Almost every at-home mother mentioned that quality time comes because she is there when her children need her. This leads some mothers to have a hard time blending their professional life with their home life, so they choose one over the other rather than trying to mesh the two. While these women were proud of their careers, held high expectations for themselves, and surprised themselves by their decision to stay home, they elected to leave the workforce because their lives were too chaotic. They now have the same pride in raising their children and attending to their families as they did attending to their past professions.

Several of these women were older mothers at high levels of management, well over age thirty, when they had their first child. Prior to having children, they worked regularly from 8 a.m. until 8 p.m. Coordinating a family with these long hours seemed insurmountable. Earning income for eight or more years before having children also gave these women the financial means to be *able* to stay at home, even if they had to cut back on their expenses to do so.

Nicole explains it well. "Once I became a mother, I left my profession because I couldn't commit 100 percent to my family and then 100 percent to my career, too. I don't have 200 percent. I didn't want to do either job partway, leaving the office early for the kids or coming home late night after night to get the latest project finished on time. I want to complete one job well, so I chose the family."

"I think that the difference between full-time employed women and stay-at-home mothers is the ability to juggle work and home. I give 100 percent to my family and 100 percent to my job," says Lisa, a former dietitian in Denver. "If I was employed, I would be thinking of one when I was with the other. It is too much stress for me to handle. I recognize that I don't handle juggling well, so I chose one over the other."

Tracy, a Midwestern at-home mother, asks, "Do you have children because you want them or just because everyone else has them? The choice is yours, and you must take on the responsibility that goes with it. The children are more important than the expensive hobby or bigger house. Raising a child is a bigger priority, so put that big house on hold. When you have a child, your life is redefined. You can grow in ways with your child that you couldn't have imagined."

Almost every stay-at-home mother reiterates how important her relationship with her family is to her. Being close to her children and her husband are among the primary reasons she is at home versus in the workplace.

"Children are quantity driven, not quality driven. If you give a kid a big shiny box versus a little plain box and tell them there is something very valuable inside the small one, the child will always pick the large shiny box," claims Dawn, a former banker. "They won't share their thoughts with you unless you spend time with them. I am always surprised at parents who don't like their children. They think that children aren't fulfilling—thank goodness that they have jobs."

"One woman that I met while on vacation at a dude ranch wanted quality time with her daughter. The daughter, however, wanted to be with the other kids at the ranch, at all the kids' special programs, not with her mother," says Ellen, a former accountant executive. "It was sad to see, but quality time comes with quantity time. You just can't tell when they will open up. You can't say, 'Hey, today I have time for you in my schedule. I will fit you in at

3 p.m.' You must be accessible because you can't get this time back. It is ironic that there is quantity over quality. There are days that my daughter, Chelsea, doesn't interact with me, but if she needs me, I'm here. I get all of the comments when Chelsea gets home from school—ten minutes later, it's lost. My husband doesn't hear it when he comes home; I have to tell him."

Mary Ann, a former physician from Texas, concurs. "As the children get older, it's even more important to be home with the teens. Things can get out of hand if you do not have your eyes and ears open all the time. I'm there to listen to my kids and my kids' friends because many of my children's friends' parents are not always there."

"When I was working part time, I picked up my child at 2 p.m.," says Paula, a former chemist. "If the other mothers had seen the looks on their children's faces, it would have broken their hearts. After school, kids love to go home. A friend's daughter was thrilled that her mother lost her job because now she gets to go home with her."

"It really matters that you bond with your kids when they are young," asserts Corey, a former real estate agent. "My son talks to me daily from college. His friends are jealous that he has such a good relationship with his parents, while they don't."

There are some mothers that had so much trouble conceiving that when they either get pregnant or adopt a child, they are so thankful to have children that they want to be intimately involved with every aspect of their child's life. "I have an adopted son, and he is so important to me that I have never worked full time after he came to our home. I'm lucky to have the ability to stay home," claims Cheryl, a former nurse from Ohio.

Smooth-Running Household

Many of the at-home mothers note how much smoother their family life runs when they stay home, claiming that "life is better for my whole family when I stay at home." Family life is not as disorganized when Mom gets chores done and errands completed during the day, enabling her to get the kids to afternoon activities, have dinner on the table at a reasonable hour, and aid in homework assignments at night. Liz sums it up for many: "Quality of life for some people means a luxury car and expensive vacations, but to me, it's sitting down at dinner together as a family and not living in constant chaos."

"Now I get more done at home," says Mary Ann. "I used to leave the breakfast dishes on the table and clean them up right before dinner. Now I have a sense of pride holding a home together. To me, it's heroic to have a great home as I never thought that I had these skills—I was always an intellectual."

"The house is clean, dinner is made, and I'm not doing the laundry at 10 p.m. at night," claims Emily, a former advertising director from New Jersey. "I have a full-time employed friend who came over to my house on the spur of the moment to fill containers full of water and bathe her children because the water main had broken on her street after lunch that day. She visited in the late afternoon as I was just finishing the dinner preparations. The table was set, the house was clean, dinner was in the oven, and my daughter was doing her homework in the family room. She looked around my house then broke down and cried, saying that she had no water, the breakfast dishes were still on the kitchen table, her house was a disaster area, all the clothes needed washing, and that the family would be lucky to get Kentucky Fried Chicken for dinner. I felt so bad for her because, by contrast, my family life is so much smoother and under control due to my being home all day."

Elsie, a former Wall Streeter, says, "When my husband is gone, he can focus 100 percent on his job. He is not worrying that the bills aren't being paid, that the kids are sick, or that the plumber needs to be let in mid-morning—I do it all. My being at home helps him to focus on his career. His job is bringing in the money, while mine is totally running the household—home repairs, yard work, food preparation, financial management, coordinating the children's activities. . . . We both have better lifestyles by my staying at home, otherwise both of us would be going crazy trying to get it all done."

Discipline

"Sometimes I feel that working parents are almost afraid to discipline their children because they are not with them very much," asserts Rachael. "They want to be their children's friends more than they want to be their parents. Children, especially teens, need boundaries, and those boundaries must be set by their primary caregivers, namely, the parents. As an at-home mother, I punish my children for wrongdoings. They had time-outs when they were young, and now they lose privileges such as Internet time in their teen years. It takes time and energy to correct a child and then even more endurance to carry through consistently on penalizations. As an employed mother, I just don't think that I would have the strength to battle my teens and keep them in line."

Although not discussed as in-depth as other topics, discipline is an important part of being home for numerous mothers. By having more time available with the children, these parents are not apprehensive about punishing their children for misdeeds.

Georgette agrees with Rachael on the issue of discipline. "Sometimes I feel like I'm 'the mean mother.' I have a musical therapy degree, and I have seen what a lack of discipline does to children in the behavioral disorder room at my former place of employment. It's simple to get kids to do the right thing if you are willing to put the effort into it. I know that I am more strict with my children than the daycare providers would be. If the children get their work done, they can go out and play with their friends. My children know the rules, and this frees me of yelling. One example of carrying out the rules is the day when my four-year-old and six-year-old made a big mess in their rooms with their clean clothes. They threw all the neatly folded clothes up in the air and all around the room. I told them if they ever did that again they would have to do the laundry for a week. They did it again a few days later and guess what? I made them do the laundry for a week. My friends were aghast at the idea, but it works. They must learn at a young age or they will never learn."

"When I was working as a pharmacist, I didn't always say, 'No, you can't do this, and, no, you can't do that.' It was a bit like a three-ring circus with my husband, and I was just letting it happen," explains Denise. "I didn't want to discipline them during the few precious hours a day that I saw them. And when I first stayed home, I wondered, 'Where did the fun mommy go?' I couldn't be the 'fun' mom with the three-ring circus continuing all day. I had to adjust to the situation, as did my children. We grew into my new role together. Now we see a better side of each other all the time."

"Coming from a family of teachers, I hear about wild children at school all the time. It is easy to see which parents are involved with their kids' lives," claims Anne, vice president of a promotions company. Her husband is a stay-at-home dad. "When kids are wild, I wonder if they're coming from a two-parent-income household."

Relocation

"My husband and I have moved six times in fourteen years," says Liz, former money manger. "With all that moving, I'm the only constant in my children's lives. I have given up things for the family and chosen to be the continuity for my children. With each move, I kept the same schedule for the kids to give them as much stability as possible. I couldn't have done that and worked simultaneously. If it wasn't for the kids, I would still be employed with a financial institution. With each move, I usually settle the kids into school, get the house together, and then decide what to do with myself. Several times I've just gotten myself a part-time job and then boom—we move again."

Mobility in our society, particularly corporate and military relocations, has created situations where career-oriented parents conclude that one parent bowing out of the workplace is in the best interest of the children. Surprisingly, about one-third of the at-home mothers I interviewed decided to stay home with the children because they have relocated so many times. With the disruption of schools, friends, and neighborhoods, these moms provide the stability for their children by being at home. In two of the interview situations where the mother is the major breadwinner in the family, Dad decided to stay home with the children amid all the moves so that he provides the continuity in the family. No matter who stays home, both parents are confident that having one of them as the primary caregiver at home helps smooth the transition for the children.

"With the eight moves I have made in nine years due to my husband's corporate job, my kids have gotten consistent discipline and a good, moral foundation on life because I left the workplace to stay at home with them." Emily, a former advertising director, continues, "It was tight at the beginning, but one of us wanted to interact with the children and discipline them, making our lives as sane as possible. The kids know Mom will be there with the same routine and same schedule no matter where we live."

Former insurance manager Helen adds, "With each of the nine moves that I have made in sixteen years, it was like ripping a patch off of a jacket. You had to mend your life back together. . . . It could be done, but it took time and was a little harder each time to make it turn out right. We had no friends—my kids, my husband, myself—it was stressful. I read that it takes three years to become established in a new location, having friends that you bump into at the supermarket, knowing a neighbor well enough that you can call them to pick up your son when you are in a jam, generally being comfortable in the town. We were never anywhere that long. We had infidelities, mental health issues, and marital problems with all of these moves. But through all of this, we are still together as a family. I can't imagine how much worse it would have been if I had not been at home."

Time for Self and Friends

"While working full time, I did not exercise, was not toned, had no time to myself to participate in the activities that I enjoy such as playing the piano, going to dance class, or lifting weights at the gym, even though my husband made time for himself. Mothers naturally just put themselves last in line. Everyone gets their needs fulfilled before Mom," contends Melinda.

Women having time for themselves as well as for their husbands came up again and again under the positive aspects of being a stay-at-home mother. Alone time allows mothers to perform simple, everyday activities such as exercising, reading books, knitting, shopping for themselves, baking, painting, socializing with friends, and even just napping.

"When the girls started school full time, many people automatically assumed I would go back to 'work,' from friends to family," says Betty. "When I'd meet people at social gatherings, and they asked, 'What do you do?' and I'd say, 'I raise twins who are six years old and in first grade.' They'd respond, 'Oh, you don't work?' Politely, I would never answer back what I was thinking, which was, 'Obviously, you've never had twins.' When the next question was, 'Now that they're in school all day (which, by the way, ended at 2:10 p.m.), you're going back to work, right?' I wanted to tell them that this was the first time in six years that I was able to be alone, to exercise, to just do simple errands without two children vying for my attention. When they went to first grade, and all the years beyond, I was still very much involved in their lives, in and out of school, but for the first time I was able to have a small amount of time for myself."

According to former secretary Patty, "I'm now more relaxed and lenient with the kids than I would have ever guessed. Spending leisure time at the pools and parks with the kids is an integral part of our weekly activities. Now that I am staying home, I'm incorporated with those I get along with, going to each other's houses, shopping at Costco together and buying hot dogs for the kids there, meeting at the park, and stopping for ice cream cones. As an employed mother, I never would have done that."

"After working full time for four years as a mother, I left corporate America. I napped for two hours every day for six months after I resigned, I was that exhausted. After I was home for a few months, my husband thought I looked ten years younger, and I felt that way," claims Beth, a former marketer.

CONS TO BEING A STAY-AT-HOME MOTHER

No more daycare compromises, no more juggling two jobs, no more living in constant chaos, plenty of time for family and self—these are the reasons women decide to resign from their occupations and stay home. Yet the at-home mother's world is not like that of June Cleaver in the late 1950s television show *Leave It to Beaver*. Today's mothers have been out in the workplace, earning their own paychecks and shouldering the responsibilities that come along with making money. Now when she remains home, she misses various aspects of her vocation—an identity, intellectual stimulation, respect for a day's work well done, and a paycheck. In addition, her routines are isolating and debilitating because of a lack of adult interaction and positive feedback.

We live in a society in which the lowest form of work, both in terms of status and finances, is day-to-day childcare. Domestic cleaning work is even more highly paid.[1] So when a woman leaves her career to become a "full-time mother," she trades in her professional identity for one that holds little social status in most people's eyes, making her feel much less empowered than when she was employed.

Nonidentity

"I use to wear a lab coat with a nametag everyday. Then, when I stayed home, it was like I hit a brick wall," claims Wisconsin mother Paula. "When you don't work, you don't have an immediate identity in today's world, forcing you to develop one yourself. People were indifferent to me when they heard that I didn't have a career. It took me a year or two to get used to not being a chemist, not having a professional identity."

Stemming from the 1950s when the father was the breadwinning head of the household, and the mother was the "little woman," the imagery of a stay-at-home mother being insecure and incapable of holding down a job still perseveres today, making it difficult to form a positive at-home identity when one is "just a mother." Susan Lewis, author of *Reinventing Ourselves after Motherhood*, states, "The problem of identity that hounded women in 1963 still plagues us at the millennium, in part because many of us mistook men for our role models and job titles for our identities. Under such circumstances, when the job title departs, so goes our sense of self."[2]

"During my years of employment, I had always paid someone else to clean my house and wash the clothes, but now, after resigning, I do it all myself," says Helen. "About one month after stopping my occupation, I spent the whole day cleaning and straightening up the house. When my husband arrived home, I asked him, 'Did you notice what I did today?' I had to justify my existence. He always had understood my conversation regarding major presentations at the office, but when I tried to explain this cleaning the house thing, why it was so important, it seemed almost pitiful to me. *This* was now my *job*. The more I tried to explain it to him, the more embarrassed I got. After becoming tongue-tied over vacuuming, dusting, and clothes washing, I felt so pathetic that I had a major meltdown. But then everything was okay after that. We spent five years with various live-in nannies and au pairs, trying to bridge the time we were at work in the best way we thought possible. Since I have been at home, I've never been happier. My biggest regret is that it took so long for me to reevaluate where our priorities were and why I had children in the first place."

Who you are is what you "do" in our society, but you aren't always sure what is expected of you when you are at home. There are no job descriptions, clear-cut schedules, or long-term goals. This lack of an affirmative identity is demeaning for many stay-at-home mothers, causing internal conflicts and demoralization. For numerous women, this is the worst aspect of staying home. Lisa summarizes it well: "No one grows up aspiring to be a stay-at-home mom."

"When we moved to Europe for my husband's career, I was forced to be an at-home mother, having my choice and computer marketing career taken away from me," says Hillary. "After a while, I was tired of being Eric's mom or Steve's wife, losing *my* identity. It was depressing and took time, but now I'm secure in who I am, having created a new identity as a stay-at-home mother, no longer needing a job to validate me."

Liz agrees with Hillary regarding being labeled by her husband, child, or husband's career. "Living in a small corporate town, the first question that everyone asks me is, 'What does your *husband* do?' I am labeled by his job if he is management or not. If he wasn't an executive, then I would be dismissed as a peon, not worth getting to know. If I don't work or have a husband in upper management, then I can't say anything worthy of others' attention. I really wish that I was employed whenever that happens."

"My dissatisfaction with my identity as a stay-at-home mom led to a midlife crisis, causing me to search for something new, almost leading to an affair," asserts Sara. "It had a large impact on my marriage. We got through it, but between his traveling and my identity issue, we had a rough time for a while."

Even some at-home mothers *themselves* envision other stay-at-home moms as boring and nonintellectual. They don't see themselves as the at-home mothers that they are but as former professionals taking time off to raise their children. No wonder stay-at-home moms have issues of selfhood.

"When people ask me what I do, I still say that I am on a two-year leave of absence. . . . Saying you are a stay-at-home mom is a conversation stopper—it says you are a freeloader and don't do anything. I was proud of my career, great house, family, and being a wife. I was doing it all, but then again I was also burnt into the ground," says Julie. "When I left, my neighbors assumed that I was downsized. They postulate when you cannot do anything else, you become a stay-at-home mother, even though they are stay-at-home mothers themselves. That's why at-home moms have identity problems."

Some at-home mothers actually hide their backgrounds from other stay-at-home moms, thinking that their education and past workplace experience may alienate them from their friends. They are apprehensive that they may be accused of "bragging" about their past identities much in the same way that they perceive currently employed mothers "boasting" about their careers.

Mary Ann, previously a full-time physician, divulges, "I went from being boss woman and, by the way, making a salary two to three times my husband's, to becoming 'Mrs. Doctor.' I slipped into the role, hiding who I had been. One friend caught me when I was taking my son to the pediatrician. I said to him, 'Daddy is a doctor, too, you know.' My friend said, 'Why didn't you tell him that you are also a doctor?' I don't know why I'm not telling people my background, but I'm not. I am keeping it to myself."

Donna, a partner in a Massachusetts recruiting firm, says that at-home mothers have confidence issues when returning to the workforce after being unemployed for five or ten years. "Mothers at home lose their edge and think that they are worth very little in the marketplace when they really are quite valuable. They don't think that they can play with the big boys anymore and so must be built back up again. I have them put their volunteer work on the resumes. That's hard work, lots of sweat, and equity without pay. Women, particularly at-home mothers, sell themselves short."

"I gave up nursing, making my life all about my children," says Cheryl. "I sometimes wonder if I'm losing the concept of who I am. When the last child goes off to school, what will my new role be? I will have to redefine myself, and I'm not sure how easy that will be."

Susan Chira, a *New York Times* journalist and author of *A Mother's Place*, believes that we have confused the idea of devotion with sacrifice. Devotion is an offering of motherhood, but the sacrificial mother has lost all sense of self. Those very sacrifices that society claims create a "good mother" may make the at-home mom unhappy and ineffective and may eventually poison her.[3]

"My theory is that there are two types of at-home mothers—those who have chosen to stay home, raising their children while also pursuing other personal interests, or those who just stay home period," states Colleen. "You must have a stake in something other than your children. You must do something for yourself, such as join a book club, participate in an activist group, aid a charity, contribute time at church or temple, volunteer at your children's schools, or sign up for an art class. It is a shame if you lose yourself as an individual because there will be a time when your kids will not need you anymore, and then where will you be? You must have other interests beyond the family. You can't lose sight of that."

Lack of Intellectual Stimulation

"I was a high achiever, very successful at what I did. I gained self-esteem from that as clients thanked me, recognizing me as a good worker. But as a stay-at-home mother, I have no intellectual stimulation—a piece of me is missing, my spirit," says Pamela. "Being a volunteer is just boring to me. An energy, a passion comes out when I work, and I have yet to find it at home. I don't click with the hard-core, artsy-craftsy stay-at-home mothers I meet at school. I have found no best friend."

"While attending a playgroup when I first became an at-home mom, all the mothers discussed the merits of a new Tide package! AGH! Talk about wasting time and talent," Hillary says. "I relate best to those who had high-powered jobs in the past, even though they are staying home now. They're more interesting."

Expressing their disillusions of having to wrestle with voids of intellectual conversations, many mothers voice a longing for the exhilaration and fervor that they received from an occupation. This is the second hardest part of staying home, the lack of consistent, invigorating adult dialogue and the revitalization gained from it.

Many of these women have labored to have careers, so now, when they are no longer at the office, they have this huge, super-charged enthusiasm aimed directly toward their families and, specifically, their children. They are being frustrated in that effort, groping with the sense that they are "all dressed up with nowhere to go." They may be blocked by an invisible barrier that they have to overcome—it is all about use of energy and intellect, wanting to change things for the better, and discovering the best path for them to take.

"I feel a camaraderie, a sisterhood with at-home mothers. Yet sometimes, I feel that my world is too small—just talking about nothing except PTA issues drives me crazy. I want to talk beyond costs of playground equipment, issues with music assemblies, those everyday life issues. Occasionally, I change the direction of conversations by starting discussions about books or recent current events," states Jo Ann.

Betty agrees. "Now that my girls are fourteen years old, I am realizing how important it still is for me to be there for them. And although I don't regret my decision made years ago, there have been many times over their childhood when I longed for adult conversations and ways to use my mind creatively."

Isolating, Debilitating Routines

"I must do more than just the day-to-day as I am miserable after having a nice career. There's a ton of tedious housework—cleaning, cooking, laundry—I find it boring. After fifteen years of working, I must have another outlet. I have two beautiful homes, a boat, a great husband . . . but something is missing; there is no spark. I'm so depressed. Do you know what I hate most? It is coming downstairs to a clean dishwasher every morning. It symbolizes the tedious, repetitive housework that I will have to do all day. I get no sense of accomplishment out of it," says Pamela.

Pamela speaks for many women who find time at home isolating, unbearable, and debilitating because of the lack of daily adult interaction, the absence of a long-term goal, and the scarcity of positive feedback regarding their chores. One-third of the stay-at-home mothers interviewed claim that their mundane schedules, along with the drudgery of housework, is what they like least about their lives today. When employed, one is constantly meeting other adults; handed goals of various levels from their employers, if not outlining the goals themselves; and given feedback via reviews and raises. Since mothers have held occupations prior to staying home, they miss these things. Using their organizational skills to ensure that the laundry is put away, the food is bought, and the house is clean saps the energy of many women. Getting to know like-minded people is arduous because mothers do not have a built-in network from which they can build friendships. The workplace has social circles of people with similar interests, but by staying home, women connect with people randomly, making it difficult to develop friends.

This does not sound much different than what Betty Friedan wrote in 1963: "Each suburban wife struggled with it alone. As she made the beds, shopped for groceries, matched slipcover material, ate peanut butter sandwiches with her children, chauffeured Cub Scouts and Brownies, lay beside her husband at night—she was afraid to ask even of herself the silent question—'Is this all?'"[4] It still remains true today for many mothers.

Beth is one of those mothers. "I am the 'Queen of the Thankless Tasks.' My husband only notices my efforts if there is a dirty heap of unwashed laundry in the bathroom or his dry cleaning is not back yet or the breakfast and lunch dishes have piled up in the sink. I miss people at work and fulfillment—my brain is going to mush because I have little kids at home. At first, it was gratifying having a nice dinner on the table every night, but now I'm not enjoying being home as much. You are cooped up all day, cleaning; chauffeuring children to and from nursery school; preparing breakfast, then lunch, then dinner; wiping down the dog coming in and out of the rain. It's not just going to breakfast and having coffee with the girls."

"When I was working full time, I had a stay-at-home neighbor who ran over to my house with her child the second I pulled my car in the driveway every day," says Corey. "This was frustrating as I wanted a chance to unwind and time alone with my daughter. Now that I stay home myself, I understand that she was desperate to interact with someone."

Sara agrees that being home is much different than she had imagined. "I thought staying home was a cushy job until I stayed home. It takes all day to do laundry, clean, mow the grass, and play with the children. . . . I was always envious of mothers at home with their kids, but I underrated how hard it is to stay home with the children all day and *then* all night. I underestimated the mental challenge being home all day with young children."

"While I was in sales, I had a hectic, fast-paced life, so when I resigned, it was like running into a brick wall. I just stopped," says Diane. "When selling, I was always visiting customers, always on the phone to clients. People were looking for me and wanted my opinion. I miss that positive feedback and constant customer interaction."

Lacking a list of daily accomplishments bothers many mothers who were interviewed. Again, some of this stems from their occupational disciplines. "Staying home is a frustrating routine for someone from the working world. I can't check off the boxes. I can't clear the room to focus on my work. I can't hand off work to another department or another peer. Now, I have learned that checking items off my list is not as important as it was, but that doesn't alleviate the frustration," states Ellen, a former account executive.

Denise, a former pharmacist, agrees. "Checking items off of the list, that is what I like to see, yet at home I get one and a half things done off of a list of five. Now, I have low expectations, but it took me a year to get there. There are bad days—like when my husband gets home at 7 p.m. since the children start to act up every day just as I begin preparing supper around 5 p.m. Cooking dinner with such little ones, a one-year-old and a three-year-old, is impossible. Getting meals on the table is just one example of the difficulty of getting things done, so I have adjusted my expectations."

Devoid of Respect

"Men have a similar perspective of at-home mothers that full-time employed moms have, that stay-at-home mothers are lazy and sit around all day. Shame on people for not thinking that raising the next generation is significant! There's value in what everyone does. People place esteem in what they can see and touch, not in all the daily, small, invisible deeds. These acts are only judged when they are incomplete or unfinished. Playing games with the kids isn't respected as it has nothing to do with money or production," claims Holly.

The aim of the feminist movement was to give equal rights to women and men, to give women the ability to embrace an occupation, *not* to demand that women pursue a profession. It was about *choices*, not *requirements*. Most stay-at-home mothers make their home and family their career, shifting their energies from employment to home just as they would switch their energies from an old employer to a new one. Taking their role as solemnly as professional employment, they have high expectations of themselves. As Tracy, a former environmental engineer, asserts, "Now it is twisted—if you do not have a career, you are less than you should be. I want to be respected for staying at home."

"Initially, when I resigned from a large corporation to stay home with my three children, I felt as though I wasn't contributing to society. My neighbors, friends, and relatives didn't say anything regarding this—it came from within me. It took several years to get over that . . . to feel as though I was still smart and contributing to society, but in a different way," says Hillary. "Let's face it, what I had done in my previous career was not changing the world, yet, because it was for pay, it seemed more important. I know now, of course, that it wasn't."

"Some days seem so thankless," claims Beth. "My husband has actually walked in and said, 'Isn't the laundry done?' It would be like me saying to him, 'Can't you make more money?' We are completing our jobs to the best of our abilities."

Because mothers' daily tasks are seen more when they are left undone rather than when completed—such as washing the bathroom towels, vacuuming the carpets covered in dog fur, and picking up shoes from all over the house—they appear almost invisible. In addition, since mothers at home don't report to a place of employment during set hours, on the surface they seem to always be available. The combination of these facets of the stay-at-home mother's life makes her the "put upon" one. If something is amiss or goes wrong or breaks, she is the one expected to drop everything and be there. Being seen as the one who can drop everything even further diminishes the value of her job, adding to the stress of being undervalued.

"If things happen unexpectedly in the family, I'm the backup . . . I smooth things out . . . I'm the 'accommodator.' Mothers who introduce priorities for themselves into the family situation must have an amazingly secure and understanding marriage," asserts Nicole. "It's hard to be there all the time, always dropping everything to give priority to the children, husband, and home."

Heather, a part-time publisher, has another name for this stress. "Changing the stay-at-home image is hard, as the mother at home presents herself and her home as perfect. She almost wants to present the image that it is done easily. Unknowingly, it convenes the idea that she has time on her hands when, in reality, she does not. She is expected to be perfectly rested, have on the perfect makeup, be perfectly slender, and have the perfect house. She is burdened by these expectations. Barely having time to get it together, she then gets cold water thrown in her face by employed mothers asking, 'What do you do all day?' I call this 'picture perfect' stress as she is facing the attitude that she is just 'at leisure' whether she is in an affluent community or not.

"The suburban lifestyle for mom is seen as an easy one—grab a cup of coffee and chat with your girlfriends despite the fact that she is running an institution called home," she continues. "She's the glue that keeps it all together. The income is so high in some communities that it is assumed that someone else is doing all the manual labor for her. While some *do* have sufficient means to have cleaning help, the wife is still doing all the cooking, grocery shopping, laundry, driving the children from activity to activity, and the managerial work."

Shari's final statement to me summarizes it for many others. "I'm sad to say that society values good character for so little; wives and mothers get little respect. When you try to do a genuinely good job—cooking a dinner from scratch versus throwing a TV dinner in the microwave, decorating and cleaning the house versus leaving the place a mess, sitting with your child while she slowly, ever so slowly, reads her first few books out loud—and then you hear, 'Is that all you do?' It's really painful to us. Society is sending a loud, detrimental message, 'If you don't get paid for it, it must not be very important.' It's why so many moms are now afraid to stay home. Being a good mother is one of the most meaningful positions a woman can hold, yet it receives no pay and no respect."

Guilt regarding Money

According to Ann Crittenden, in the twentieth century, "'work' or 'labor' became synonymous with cash income and with 'men's' work. The stage was set for the assumption—still with us—that men 'supported' their wives at home, as if unpaid work were not productive and not part of the 'real' economy."[5] Mentioning money brings up guilt with several at-home mothers. Since they are not bringing home a paycheck, some feel worthless in today's society, and others are wary of spending too much money, women you might call "cheap." Squeezing every nickel is one way to compensate for not earning an income. Others have mentioned that they occasionally worry, "What would I do about money if something happened to my spouse?" Lack of financial security and recent job skills creates a sense of guilt as well as nervousness. As one mother said, "I have a life, but I regret not having financial security."

"Even though my neighbors eat pizza and Burger King weekly for dinner, I only order food out when I'm in a panic situation. I just can't justify spending money on take-out food when I don't have a job," claims Cheryl. "There are plenty of days when I'm out of the house all day, running errands, leading Girl Scout meetings, or volunteering at church, but I still come up with something for the family from my refrigerator."

Not only do some mothers staying home feel guilty regarding money, but a few resent their lack of financial freedom. Rachael is one of them. "My husband earns the money and controls it as well. He gives me enough to buy the groceries, household items, and the children's clothing. But if a big bill comes in, I'm yelled at even if it is something beyond my control such as a furnace repair. I sometimes wish that I worked so I could spend my earnings as I please . . . buying little extra things that men do not appreciate, such as fresh flowers or a cake from the bakery without my husband's consent."

WHAT MAKES IT WORK

Reviewing the list of cons for stay-at-home mothers—a lack of identity, the absence of intellectual stimulation, and a life devoid of respect as well as monotonous, lonely routines—one begins to wonder whether there are *any* happy, satisfied stay-at-home mothers out there. According to mothers themselves, watching the house and the children to the exclusion of everything else causes them to become "snippy and bitchy." By limiting themselves to the home, they are frustrated with their lives and, sometimes, are soured on life because they were trained for far more and realize that they are not fully utilizing their skills.

The good news is that there *are* lots of content and fulfilled at-home mothers. Focusing on issues beyond maternal ones and getting out of the house makes at-home life satisfying and gratifying. At-home mothers believe that the "good life" is not necessarily related to material goods—it is about having time to pursue personal interests such as environmental concerns, classes where mothers learn new skills, charity work, or exercise routines while having plenty of time for the family as well. And these women carry little guilt because most are contributing to society as volunteers at organizations such as schools, town boards, charities, or religious affiliations. Many are also handling the family's finances, allowing them to share in the monetary aspect of the marriage.

Volunteering

Forming an identity around volunteer work is fulfilling for many mothers at home. While they are not earning income, this gives them a meaningful role in society beyond motherhood. Their volunteerism supports communities, hospitals, religious groups, national associations of all types, and schools. Emily's words are the same as those of numerous mothers: "I felt sheepish and intimidated when I first stayed home but now am comfortable and have a sense of direction and purpose. My volunteer work is a big part of that."

Wendy Kaminer, author of *Women Volunteering*, describes it best: "Volunteering was hardly a daring choice for modern American women, but it still represented a conscious attempt to balance domestic life with work. By choosing a volunteer career, a woman was not simply choosing home and family; she was acknowledging that, although it came first for her, family life and social activities that went with it were not enough. . . . For her, volunteering has been a kind of halfway house between the family and society. It may not have gained her the world, but at least made her part of it."[6]

And the largest recipients of these efforts are the school systems all over the country, over 90 percent of the at-home mothers interviewed assist schools by giving them part of their week. Time is spent in the classrooms teaching art appreciation, helping students edit their compositions on the computer, listening to individual young children read aloud, and leading party activities throughout the year. In addition, mothers run the parent-teacher organizations that plan special student assemblies, organize authors to present to the schools, produce newsletters regarding recent or upcoming events at the schools, and raise funds for upgrading school materials such as library books, musical equipment, or playground apparatus.

"Meddling in education is an outlet for me as I can't just stay home. I dropped everything to stay home for my children, but that alone was not enough, so education is my purpose now. Many other mothers I know also feel the same way; it is a great resource for schools to harness," claims Denise.

Helen observes the same behavior in her area. "In my town, every committee in the PTA is more than it has to be because at-home mothers are channeling their energy into that job; it is what invigorates them. For some of these mothers, it is their outlet, replacing the work environment."

"Performing deeds relating to reading has been gratifying to me. I developed a list of books which are good for parents to read to their children and sent the list home via the PTA newsletters," says Molly. "Then, I brought new books from the public library to the elementary school for the kids to read and review. We published the written reviews in the local newspaper, giving the kids a thrill and encouraging them to read more."

While work for education-related purposes is far and away the most mentioned volunteer job, there are other organizations, including churches, temples, sports clubs, or charities for the homeless or abused, where stay-at-home mothers spend their time.

Molly's account is just one of the gratifying volunteer stories told to me. "Many times, children of parents who have substance-abuse problems aren't given proper care because of the parents' issues. Some of these parents are committed to changing and, while they are in the process, need help with their children, so I established volunteer foster care outside of protective services. I helped to set up a licensed group foster home and ran it for five years. The first four children that came in were siblings and had one pair of shoes between all of them. Prior to setting up this group foster home, I took these children into my own home. I had fourteen children rotate through my house in one year—this was in addition to my own five children. I never thought that I could be a teacher because I had no patience, but look at me now."

Molly continues, "My volunteer work includes the Board of Candlelighters, summer camp for kids with cancer, Historical Foundation Board, Academic Boosters Board [which provides scholarships to smart kids, not just athletes], Liturgy of the Word for Children at church, and I take communion to a nursing home once a month. This sounds so busy, yet it is not for me because I am a lousy housekeeper—I would rather be out helping others than dusting. I also cook food for the priests and bring in food after funerals. When I look over my life, I had extra energy when the kids were small, and Play-Doh did not cut it for me. At the end of the day, I wanted to accomplish something that felt significant to me. That's why I continue to volunteer for so many organizations."

Obviously, Molly considers volunteer work her career and is a master at it. While most women are not as dedicated to charity work as she is, many mothers view helping volunteer organizations as their way to "make a difference" and "accomplish meaningful tasks" beyond the everyday, routine chores of being a mother.

Colleen is another one of those women. "I am an avid volunteer at the church, chair the preschool board, cook for various church events, and plan camp sessions. There's a family camp that takes a year to plan, obtaining the speakers and putting the children's programs together. That takes a lot of my time. I also volunteer at school to fill schedules for reading and tutoring for reading and math. Since I've trouble obtaining enough mothers to work on some of the days, I fill in with my own time quite a bit. In addition, my daughter figure skates, so I help out in the ice rink, checking contracts and playing the music. I stay there the entire practice because I live forty-five minutes away, and it makes no sense to drive back home so that I can just turn around again to pick her up. In fact, I'm there helping out so much that they offered to *pay* me."

"Grant writing for the Junior League was fulfilling work for me," explains Paula. "Since I had no experience in the field, the Junior League paid for me to take a course in grant writing. One grant was for renovating a building to become a family center in an impoverished area where there were drugs and a lack of education. Once the building was opened, a high school equivalency program was offered as well as classes in computer skills. Another grant was for obtaining furniture for the homeless as they acquired homes. That program ran for five years. Other volunteer work included being a den leader for the Boy Scouts, holding a garage sale for my temple on eBay, and providing art enrichment for children at an elementary school."

Patty asserts that volunteer work helps with her self-esteem. "While I'm not working, I still need a boost or pat on the back, someone to say, 'Job well done.' I have received trophies for being the 'best new neighbor.' It sounds silly, but everyone needs positive reinforcement once in a while."

Although almost every at-home mom interviewed gains satisfaction from volunteering, a few mothers' ventures into volunteer work were not positive. It's not the ultimate answer to intellectual stimulation and social interaction for everyone.

The outcome of Dawn's good intentions did not meet her original goals. "The well-educated mothers fill their time with school volunteer work, even though the schools want your time, not your mind. I was PTA president for two years, hoping to change things in my son's parochial school, whose church we also attended. The administration always wanted to do things a certain way 'because this is the way we have always done it' and was resistant to any change. Because of this opposition to modifications, we ended up leaving the school and the parish as well."

Melinda also had a negative experience with her volunteer hours. "As a patient liaison volunteer at the hospital, the nurses and administration and doctors acted as if I was in the way, as if I was an imposition. You would think that the hospital did not want the help the way we were treated, yet every week there was a listing in the newspaper asking for patient liaison volunteers. This work was in the city hospital where there were constant shootings and knifings. The volunteers' jobs were to help out the friends and families who were stressed out over their loved ones. People in the waiting room were grateful for our help, but in the treatment area the doctors and nurses were awful to us. I only made it volunteering there one year before I said, if I'm going to put up with this, I will get paid for it. This work for me was like being a preschool teacher or daycare worker, filling a necessary job that is providing an excellent service yet getting treated poorly and paid little."

Socializing with Friends

"At-home mothers are looking for companionship during the day. Initially, I socialized with mothers of my children's friends. Yet as my children grew and I met more and more at-home mothers, I realized how many intelligent, intriguing mothers were in my town. Now when I interact with at-home moms, it isn't about mothering as it was when my children were younger; it isn't about being thrown together because of sports or kids activities, but it's about *my* interests," says Ellen.

While employed mothers interact with adults at the workplace, at-home moms must make an *effort* to visit or socialize with other at-home mothers. Small children tie them close to home, so stay-at-home moms must strive to cultivate friendships in order to mingle with other adults. Many of the at-home mothers with young children get together for playgroups or gather in the park, generating great comrades. By meeting regularly and going out together, they relieve that "isolated" feeling and keep their sanity while singing the ABCs for the twentieth time.

"Neighborhoods are a safe place to meet other mothers and build friendships while gaining playmates for the children. Without a neighborhood, it's much harder to get to know people. You don't have the same sense of community," declares Sara. "You must be outgoing as an at-home mother, or you will go crazy knocking around your house alone all day. Mother's Day Out was a great salvation for me as I met many other mothers that way."

Tracy concurs. "I have a few really good friends, particularly those whose husbands are gone a lot like mine. You need a support system and someone to talk to when you are left alone with the kids, day in and day out, especially when the children are all under age five, like mine. It's great that we are all in the same position so we can help each other out. I had my friend's children at my house for two days so that she could go away with her husband and not worry about the kids. She was so appreciative and will help me out in the future when I am in need."

"My friends and I get together on regular schedule and have mutual interests. Even though some friends are ten years older than I am, all are former professionals and older mommies. . . . I have found my niche," says Elsie. "Some full-time employed mothers say that they would be bored at home, but you just get innovative: get away to a museum, learn local folklore, venture out to the library, play a new instrument, join the YWCA, lead an apple-picking expedition . . . create new experiences for yourself, your children, and your friends!"

She continues, "Trying to balance being the in and out of the home, that is what the stay-at-home mother is doing. She does the same things day in and day out, seven days per week: laundry, cooking, cleaning, picking up after everyone else around the house. She is alone a lot, so she has to engage in activities to get her out of the house, interacting with others and not getting burnt out on the in-home routine."

Self-Directed Projects

"I have to focus, to keep myself challenged and must have a long-term goal, or I'm very unhappy," claims Sheila. "My hobby is body building and power lifting. It engages me, giving me something to strive for daily."

Sheila is not alone with her desire to constantly better herself, pushing herself in new directions; I heard this from many at-home moms. Women set out projects and timelines for themselves much as they would in a professional situation, with plans ranging from reading a book to writing a book, from redecorating a room to rebuilding a room, or from organizing one elementary school art class to developing an weeklong adult painting seminar.

Each woman sets objectives at different levels based on her available time, personal interests, age of her children, and support from friends and family.

"Being a goal-oriented person myself, I used to think, 'What do those women do at home all day?' when I worked full-time," admits Holly. "Now, having been home for a few years myself, I understand that mothers at home have long-term objectives and accomplishments because of constant interruptions all day long with children. I can't tick off daily accomplishments like I did at the office; I outline projects for myself that will take three or six months to complete."

Sometimes the goals are related to volunteering, such as maintaining the presidential position of the Parent Teacher Organization for two years, but many times they are not. Cheryl explains, "I tried to join the PTA and the Women's Club in town when I stopped working, but they were not for me. In volunteer work, women are more laid back than in an office environment. After all, they are not being paid, so things slip sometimes. I can't hold my tongue and am so outspoken that I knew people would hate me because I would tell them how to improve their operation, so I chose to do things where I will not be obnoxious."

When Rachael went back for her master's degree in teaching, her kids thought she was "cool." When Sally began faux painting inside her home, all her neighbors asked her to help them out with ideas for their homes. When Beth started photographing children in the neighborhood as birthday gifts for her friends, people began offering her money for her portraits. When Melinda's power walking helped her to lose ten pounds over six months, her daughter asked to join her twice a week. These women's personal objectives positively affected not only them but also those around them, causing a synergistic effect.

Part-Time Work

Up to now, I have written this book as if the world were black or white—either mothers are employed or not, when in actuality many mothers are employed part-time. For some, part-time employment satisfies the same role that volunteerism does for others. Based on the interviews, those who are employed twenty-five hours per week or less see themselves more as stay-at-home mothers with jobs on the side, even if the occupations are as loan officers at banks or as university professors. These employment opportunities give moms intellectual stimulation, social activity, and a feeling that they are contributing to society while not detracting from family time.

"I consider myself an at-home mom, not a working mom, as I am employed twenty hours per week," declares Cynthia, a consultant. "Since I maintain flexible hours and work from mostly home, I am constantly in the house and feel as if I'm a stay-at-home mother with a very busy schedule. I think that I have struck a balance by working part-time because my home is under control, and yet I still am fulfilling my personal ambitions."

Since there is so much to say regarding the part-timer, I have devoted chapter 6 to the topic. More exploration of her needs, schedules, and contentment will be covered in that chapter.

Involved in Finances

While those looking in from the outside may think that these women live in unequal marriages, a majority of couples have a nontraditional understanding that each person's role is indispensable for the family, with money being an irrelevant scorekeeper. The wife's role is appreciated and valued by the husband as evidenced by her either investing his income, refinancing the house, or overseeing major renovations on the home without his intervention.

"My husband comes home and hands his paycheck to me, knowing full well that I will handle all the money for the family," says Sally. "He has no financial sense and would spend everything if it were not for me. I keep track of household expenses and handle our investments. In fact, my financial prowess has resulted in our having enough funds to finish our basement as a playroom for the kids. He thinks that when he receives his bonus that we can go on a big vacation, and *I* have to explain to *him* how some of that money must be set aside for taxes and buying of furniture over the next year."

Sheila adds, "I have refinanced our home three times in the last ten years, just checking in with my husband to tell him the latest interest rates. I was the one who suggested moving into a fifteen-year mortgage when the rates were low, saving us thousands in interest payments."

An article from the *Wall Street Journal* states, "Women, long the keeper of the household checkbook, are increasingly taking charge of the family investments as well." The article explains how big investment firms such as Charles Schwab, Merrill Lynch, and Lehman Brothers are launching programs specifically to attract women. In addition, "For women who gave up careers to focus on children, overseeing the family finances can help ease some of the difficult feelings women struggle with when they stop bringing home a paycheck themselves. And it is a way to stay involved in something akin to a professional pursuit."[7]

SCHEDULE OF THE REAL STAY-AT-HOME MOTHER

Unlike the current images of stay-at-home mothers being "simple" or "overly aggressive socialites/volunteers," the real, fulfilled at-home mom is an intelligent, intriguing woman who has struck a balance between maternal issues and personal interests. For mothers with school-age children, once the family is off to school and work for the day, she has a schedule brimming with activities, chores, and errands. Those with toddlers, however, schedule activities around the children, realizing that the day may go very differently than originally planned.

Georgette discusses this. "There is no such thing as spontaneity with young children. Everything must be well organized so that you have a bottle for the baby at 2 p.m. and a snack for the toddler at 3 p.m. Otherwise, all hell can break loose just as you are settling down at the pool for a warm summer afternoon. With young children, you must realize that well-planned, intended activities can fall through at the last minute. You can schedule something great, such as a journey to a blueberry patch, and one throws up as you walk out the door or another has a meltdown after being overstimulated at a friend's home earlier in the day. You learn to be flexible and make the best of what you are doing today. You grow where you are planted.

"Suspending my life until I go back to work is *not* an option, as I need a sense of who I am today," Georgette continues. "It's much easier to be in another-directed job than to stay home. I did more in a lunch hour at the office than I can sometimes do in a day at home with small children. When the children are all alive at the end of the day, there is not much to write down in my diary. But I consider it a big accomplishment because to keep going daily with five kids is a milestone. Watching children grow, making sure that things are under control and running smoothly, is satisfying to me."

A woman with school-age children keeps a very different kind of calendar. One day she may be running the vacuum at 8:30 a.m., attending a

The Reality of Being a Stay-at-Home Mother

Parent Teacher Organization meeting at 9 a.m., having coffee with a friend at 11 a.m., driving from the library to the dry cleaners to the hardware store to the grocery store from noon to 1:30 p.m. Then, she returns home for a quick bite to eat, checks the stock market, balances the checkbook, and runs a load of wash before either walking to the bus stop to greet the children or getting back in the car to pick the kids up from school. Then, she drives them to afternoon activities such as dancing, karate, piano lessons, or basketball. Arriving back home around 4:30 or 5 p.m., she begins cooking dinner while getting the children started on homework. Once dinner is prepared, eaten, and the dishes are done, this mother will bath young children and then read them a story before putting them to bed. Finally, at the day's end, she may sit down to either watch one or two television shows or read a book, if she can keep her eyes open.

Although most afternoons follow the same pattern, with the possibility of including her as the coach or leader in one or two activities, the earlier part of her day is more fluid and fluctuates daily. It can include religious organization meetings, playgroups, personal interest classes, or self-directed projects such as repainting the living room, exercise, phoning others to coordinate activities, or other types of volunteer work. Even though some of her hours are filled with thankless, "invisible" chores, she has a gratifying, well-rounded life that keeps her cheerful.

Melinda outlines her typical schedule. "Staying home is a full-time job. I use to pay someone to do all the things I do now. My day is odd as one daughter leaves at 6:30 a.m., and the other leaves at 8:30 a.m. I'm always a background person who volunteers during the day because that works best for me. I complete my household chores in the morning, paying the bills, calling the repairman, and running errands. Then, I must pick one up at school in the early afternoon and take her to the ice rink for practice, not returning home until 5 p.m., spending lots of time in the car each afternoon. No one sees that I have to make sure that by 1:30 p.m., I have everything that I need in the car to get me through the afternoon—sports equipment, snacks for the children, change of clothes, karate gear for the one who gets picked up and then dropped off again, dry cleaning to be dropped off, and videos to be returned as well as the grocery list so I can buy food while the kids are at their classes. All these details are in my brain. Then, I get home at 5 p.m. and prepare dinner while ensuring that homework is getting done. I wash the laundry at 6 a.m. and run the dryer late at night. My husband travels a lot, so

THE WALL BETWEEN WOMEN

I can never count on him for anything. I can't volunteer or go to night meetings because I would end up getting a baby-sitter, which I can't afford to pay sitters for volunteer work."

Lisa is so happy now as a stay-at-home mother that she hopes to never return to the office. "That's so surprising to me! I can't believe that I'm saying this because, when I stopped working, I thought that this was temporary. I've always been employed—I even worked my way through school. After that, I worked for ten years and was sure that I would miss it as it was a large part of my identity, but I'm shocked by how I am content being someone's 'Mommy' and running the home."

Susan Lewis summarizes the reality of the stay-at-home mother well in her book *Reinventing Ourselves after Motherhood*: "I grew up thinking that intelligent, ambitious, well-educated women no longer stayed at home with children. I believed myself to be those things, and yet early in my thirties I stepped out of the practice of law and landed, not exactly feet first, in the world of diapers and playgrounds. I hadn't lost the desire for personal and professional fulfillment, yet children had added a dimension to my life that was much more significant, demanding, and compelling than I'd ever understood or imagined."[8]

NOTES

1. Jane Swigart, *The Myth of the Bad Mother: The Emotional Realities of Mothering* (New York: Doubleday, 1991), p. 100.

2. Susan Lewis, *Reinventing Ourselves after Motherhood: How Former Career Women Refocus Their Personal and Professional Lives after the Birth of a Child* (Chicago: Contemporary Books, 1999), p. 87.

3. Susan Chira, *A Mother's Place: Taking the Debate about Working Mothers beyond Guilt and Blame* (New York: HarperCollins Publishers, 1998), p. 23.

4. Betty Friedan, *The Feminine Mystique* (New York: W. W. Norton, 1963), p. 15.

5. Ann Crittenden, *The Price of Motherhood: Why the Most Important Job in the World Is Still the Least Valued* (New York: Henry Holt, 2001), p. 47.

6. Wendy Kaminer, *Women Volunteering: The Pleasure, Pain and Politics of Unpaid Work from 1830 to the Present* (Garden City, NY: Anchor Press, 1984), p. 5.

7. Hillary Stout, "The New Family Portfolio Manager: Mom," *Wall Street Journal* (February 10, 2005): D1.

8. Lewis, *Reinventing Ourselves after Motherhood*, p. XIV.

SIX

PART-TIME EMPLOYMENT: UTMOST OR DISMAL?

A thirty-hour work week with one day set aside just for the children—three days in the office, one at home, and Mondays off. Sounds good, yes? What about full-time responsibilities with 60 percent of the pay or the same job title for twelve years? How does that sound? You can clearly see the dilemma of the part-timer—family-friendly hours executing intelligent work in a stagnant position, with little chance for promotion.

American women are open to career opportunities out of the norm in order to balance vocations and family, forming this new species called part-timers, dependent on internal motivation and criteria to define their success. What amazed me while researching the Wall was the large number of part-timers that I ran across in my discussions. Thirty percent of the women interviewed maintain part-time employment. Of these part-timers, 50 percent were self-employed, 32 percent were part of small companies, and 18 percent were with large corporations.

Working anywhere from five to thirty-five hours per week performing paid services, from marketing research to nursing, from interior decorating to book-keeping, the part-timer has no image or stereotype. Most women, even part-timers themselves, can't describe her. She is a new breed of woman, one who strives to maintain a smooth family life yet also earns income for financial reasons as well as for her own self-esteem. Some perform part-time duties to stay current within their industries so that they can return full time when the children are in high school or if they incur unforeseen financial difficulties. Yet one does not hear about this woman who is trying to balance her life. Employment appears black or white—you are either a full-time worker or you are an at-home mother. Yet today's reality is not that concise, finding many women in that gray area of part-time work.

THE WALL BETWEEN WOMEN

If a part-time employed mother works less than twenty-five hours per week, she envisions herself as a stay-at-home mom with employment on the side. But if she is executing her occupation between twenty-five and thirty-five hours per week, she sees herself as a "lucky" working mother who has a small amount of extra time for her family versus the full-time, forty-hour-per-week worker. Yet no matter how many hours a women works, when asked about part-time employment, a clear majority of part-timers believe that it gives mothers the "best of both worlds" as long as the job involves "utilizing your brain." A small minority see part-time employment as the absolute worst possible situation, stemming from the fact that you have to "do it all" with even less money than full-time employment.

BEST OF ALL WORLDS

"I love part-time work—it's the best of both worlds, having an employer who is willing to give me real work and not just the leftovers while also getting to be home as the school bus pulls up the street," says Cindy from St. Louis. "My boss is great at delegating. He's willing to give me complex projects and is very patient with me as he sees what a hard worker I am. I was a vice president when I was employed full time, but I'm not climbing that ladder anymore. While I'm being challenged and getting a paycheck with my name on it, I still get home by the time my kids climb off the bus after school. Producing projects, interacting with adults—I enjoy that more than sitting at home by myself. Women generally do not talk about their jobs. When people hear that I work at a bank, they automatically assume that I am a teller because I'm a part-timer. They don't know my position at the bank, nor do they ask about it. Since I'm happy with my professional job, I don't correct them or even care what they think."

Most part-timers, stay-at-home mothers, and full-time employed moms all see part-time work as the ultimate situation for a mother. Part-timers earn income, hold a professional identity, and still have enough time to minimize the chaos in the home, participate in their children's schools, and maybe even have a chance to get together with girlfriends. These mothers have found that elusive sense of balance in their lives by bridging the gap between the worlds of "mom" and the "employment."

Balance is what makes Denise a better parent. The ten hours per week filling prescriptions as a pharmacist gives her enough adult interaction and energy to fulfill her in a holistic, emotional way. She enjoys time with her son much more now than when she was a stay-at-home mom. By pursuing her own interests and simultaneously taking care of her son, she maintains an equilibrium in her life.

Connecticut mom Peggy feels extremely blessed with her work situation, family atmosphere, and flexibility, as she is busy as a credit analyst at a local bank, a position that she enjoys. "Life is a tough balancing act, yet with my working twenty-five hours per week in a professional, flexible atmosphere close to home, I have the best of both worlds. I can have a professional life while the children are in school and still be a 'mom' in the middle of the day, if necessary. I consider this the ideal."

Even women who have almost full-time schedules—such as Elaine, a clinical drug research manager working thirty-two hours per week, and Heather, a publisher working between twenty and forty hours per week—feel those extra hours at home are precious and make a huge difference in their family lives.

According to Trish, the manager of a California software company, "Part-timers are in a class by themselves with an ideal situation, getting a balance of self-achievement, separate identity, friendships from other mothers, plus being able to go with the children on class trips and volunteer in the classrooms. They have achieved what I'm striving for. I took a step back in my career to spend more time with my children. Now I work forty hours versus eighty hours per week, receiving substantially less pay. Previously, I ran a large department and now have a much smaller staff and department. This was a conscious decision on my part. I was laid off in 2002 when the dot-com bubble burst, resulting in a recession in Silicon Valley. I made a decision to take a lesser job in order to spend more time with my family, turning down dozens of jobs at higher pay, and now earn fifty cents on the dollar versus what I was making before. I redid my priorities for my children in high school and refuse to work those eighty hours per week anymore. I go in early, don't take lunch, and leave early in order to be in the office only forty hours and still get all my tasks done.

"Essentially, I've formulated my own flex hours," she continues. "The finances are not so bad because when you have a salary above $200,000, you can easily cut down by not saving as much as before. This allows me to volunteer for the Boy Scouts, as I have two Eagle Scouts, and also teach Sunday school. While I can't find part-time work in my field at my level, I have rearranged my full-time job to capture the essence of a part-time job."

Learning to be task-oriented rather than holding a punch-clock mentality makes sense for time-crunched mothers. By cutting out water cooler discussions with co-workers, one-hour lunches, and coffee breaks, mothers function in a focused, intense environment to complete daily tasks in five or six hours rather than the standard eight, giving them time for family, chores, and recreation.

Donna, an executive recruiter in Boston, has the life Trish strives to obtain. "Part-time work gives me the ability to optimize both of my worlds. I run my own business three days per week and then spend the other two days with my children. My three-year-old loves Mommy picking her up from school. I feel lucky and fortunate that I get paid for work that makes me feel personally satisfied and fulfilled."

And a few mothers are part-timers to maintain their marketable skills for financial security beyond today's income stream. "I had a fear of quitting altogether, thinking, 'Would anyone ever hire me again?'" claims Kim, an office manager working twenty-five hours per week.

May, a supply/demand analyst for thirty hours per week, adds, "What happens if you are out of the workforce for fifteen years, and your husband leaves you? Where are you then?" The answer is part-time employment, which eliminates the issue.

Whether these mothers moved to part-time work to relieve stress in the family, to once again begin drawing a paycheck, or to have peace of mind regarding prospective jobs in the future, most are content with the result. "Part-time work is not perfect, but it is good for me," claims Natalie, a Web site designer. "Since I work part time from home here in Portland, it takes lots of discipline and time management because every minute counts. I have the personality that I can handle it, being self-directed. If my child wakes up sick, I can take the day off and then work on Saturday to make up for it. This enables me to be home after school when the kids are chatty and available for school events when necessary."

Cindy agrees. "All my professional friends have gone part time as the work environment makes it untenable to remain in the workforce full time. Corporations give the home front little support. I got tired of being 'Supermom' and enjoy floating between the two worlds of home and career."

Cokie Roberts, a news analyst for National Public Radio, says, "Putting the career on the back, or at least middle, burner in the years children are small makes a lot of sense to me. That doesn't necessarily mean staying at home full time. For me, that would have been a disaster. I need to work for my spiritual and emotional well-being and while that may not be admirable, it's true. In interim periods between jobs I've suffered genuine depression, and believe me, that's no good for the children. I was a better mother because I worked."[1]

Katie's comment wraps it up for the majority of part-timers: "Right now, I could increase my compensation substantially as an emergency planner if I shifted to full-time employment. But I won't because I have a perfect blend of career and family time."

WORST CASE POSSIBLE

"When I was a part-timer, I was responsible for 100 percent of my previous full-time job projects in addition to 100 percent of someone else's who had recently left, working 60 percent of the hours and receiving 60 percent of the pay I had formerly earned," declares North Carolinian Sally. "I was working two full jobs at 60 percent of the pay. The bank thought they were doing me a huge favor and made me feel that my job was on the line all the time. Because I needed the income, I let the bank take advantage of me for two entire years. I enjoyed the interaction with my customers but hated employment at the bank, working for smug men whose wives were at home."

While most women are pleased with part-time positions because of the life balance it offers, a few felt it was the worst of all worlds. The largest disadvantage is the hours-to-income ratio. Numerous women report stories of being compensated for significantly fewer hours than they are actually laboring. Obviously, they would prefer quitting to being taken advantage of, but the income is a necessity, and they want the shorter hours for their families, so they bite their tongues and sweat through the work. The second-most-mentioned drawback is the need to fulfill all the duties of a full-time employed mother, such as bringing in a certain level of income, *plus* all the responsibilities of the stay-at-home mother because, unlike the full-time employed mother, the part-timer is seen as having plenty of time for motherly obligations.

Ann Crittenden points out in *The Price of Motherhood* that "employers are not required to offer part-time employees equal pay and benefits for equal work. As a result, nonstandard workers earn on average about forty percent less an hour than full-time workers."[2]

"Why go part time?" says Joy, a former chemical engineer from Arizona. "You get 90 percent of the work with 60 percent of the money and no benefits. As a part-timer, you fit in nowhere; stay-at-home mothers think you are a full-time working mother, and full-time employed mothers think you are a stay-at-home mom."

"Working part time is the toughest of all worlds. You have double duty, the burden of earning income for the family as well as being the primary caregiver for the children, *and* you have all the stay-at-home mom duties, such as cleaning the house, laundry, grocery shopping, and cooking. It is the worst," declares former part-timer Colleen. "Because you are part time, everyone thinks that you have time for everything on both sides! You haven't gained anything because you are still working two jobs. It is all about trying to completely satisfy the office and the family with less hours available to everyone, hence, not really meeting anyone's full needs."

May asserts, "I'm paid to work thirty hours per week, yet I work well over forty hours. I am at the office Monday through Thursday and tell fellow employees that I don't work on Fridays. The idea is that I save Fridays to volunteer in school with the children. But I still get e-mails and calls from work on Fridays, pushing me back up to full-time hours."

According to Nadine Mockler, a partner in Flexible Resources, a firm specializing in recruiting and consulting in part-time work, "Women who don't like part-time employment are the ones who have bosses who expect full-time work with part-time hours. They are fielding calls and solving problems when they are at home. This is *not* the job they accepted. Parameters and criteria must be set up prior to accepting a part-time position, as you are a professional and should be treated as one."

And if these two disadvantages are not enough, the part-timer also has a miniscule chance of receiving a promotion. Lindsey has been a part-timer at the senior product manager level in a large medical corporation for *eleven* years. She is obviously a solid performer, as she is given timely and generous raises, but she will not be promoted as a part-timer. Another part-timer, Natasha, says that her company, a major consumer goods corporation, might promote her as long as there is no full-time person equivalent in skill or talent. Her employer asked her to sign a document stating that she understands that an analogous full-time employee will always receive a promotion over her as a part-timer.

Project engineer Irisa, who works thirty-five hours per week, believes,

Part-time Employment: Utmost or Dismal?

"Working part-time for the long term is difficult as corporations will limit the type work that they will assign you, also restricting your ability to be promoted. Even if you work part time and then come back full time after your children are in school, you have tipped off the corporation that your family is more important than your career, and you will always be thought of as being on the 'mommy track,' whether you want to be or not. In addition, when corporate downsizing comes along, part-timers are the first to go. It's frustrating for women who want to do right by their families and their careers."

Sometimes, part-timers are asked to come into the office on days that they are not usually scheduled, causing havoc with their daycare plans. Others have to pay full-time childcare center costs on part-time income because it is the only solution to obtaining stable childcare for their sons and daughters.

But despite all of these downsides, women are still drawn to part-time employment because of the life balance that it offers. "I'm jealous of part-timers," admits Ronnie, a director of procurement, "but I realize at the same time that they are giving up their career track. I would rather quit than be a part-timer because they have a tougher deal than anyone because they have two full-time jobs. I don't think that most part-timers know that they are on the 'mommy track.' They are still in the honeymoon stage with their babies. They will realize it when it is too late. Eventually, the part-timers might quit because of the dead-end nature of the job. That said, I'm still envious of them and have thought about part-time employment a few times myself because I really want to see more of my children."

UTMOST AND DISMAL SIMULTANEOUSLY

Since many women view part-time employment as the ultimate position, and some consider it dispiriting, it's no surprise that a few actually see it as the best *and* the worst rolled into one. Part-timers gain a balance between family time and a career, presenting them with mental challenges, income, and an identity, yet may be consigned to professional oblivion, with little or no chance for advancement. In exchange for a flexible schedule, women give up competitive salaries, benefits, and possibly job security.

Carly's sister, Isabelle, exemplifies this. "My sister was a stay-at-home mother for many years and was slowly going crazy. She felt underutilized as a human being by staying at home with the kids, so she returned to college and received a master's degree to teach high school math. Being confined by geographic boundaries, Isabelle accepted the only part-time high school math teaching position available to her. She celebrated when she received the job, even though it almost killed her the first year. Since Isabelle was a part-timer, the school gave her all the new classes. She never got to run the same class twice so was constantly reinventing what she did. This is not the norm for teaching. Isabelle was always in first-year class mode, never getting to reach the second or third year, when things run much more smoothly. But she couldn't be picky in a part-time professional job. Every year, she started two new classes from scratch, rarely instructing courses that she had taught before. Isabelle could not work full-time because both of her sons had large medical issues. The teaching, along with her sons, medical needs and the usual laundry, cooking, and cleaning, overwhelmed her. She found she was compromising her marriage and compromising herself as a human being. Therefore, Isabelle stopped teaching to accommodate the family's needs. Now she is less energized intellectually and much more financially stressed, but the family is moving along smoothly. The part-time teaching position was the best, as it invigorated her intellectually, but the worst regarding professional workload and family issues.

While Danielle held flexible hours versus part-time hours, she has a story similar to Isabelle's. She was employed by a large, recognizable Fortune 100 corporation that I will call Alpha. "Working flexible hours was possible for me as long as I got in forty hours per week and my assignments were completed on time at Alpha Corporation. I had two afternoons a week at home with the kids, giving me the balance that I needed to spend time with my children. When my boss left to be an at-home mother with her middle school and high school children, it made me think, why am I staying? I had never considered leaving work until this time. When my new boss arrived, she said that my flex time was over. That flexibility made all the difference in the world to me, it was so sacred! Having it taken away made me take a second look at my life, giving me a different perspective. So I decided to leave the job behind. If they hadn't removed my flexible hours, I would probably still be working there today. But I was burning the candle at both ends— the perfect mother, wife, and executive—something had to give at some point. I am thankful that my boss left and paved the way for me to leave as well. And I'm grateful for the manager who wiped away my flex time so that I could make the decision to stay at home. My ex-boss who stayed home to be with her children before they went off to college was trying to make up for the past fifteen years. Seeing this happen made it so much easier for me to leave the workforce while my children are young. It made it so easy to embrace the opportunity before me now. My husband and I always thought that he would be the first of the two of us to retire, as I was always the more ambitious one.

"It was funny because Alpha was recently honored by *Working Mothers* magazine for being terrific to full-time working mothers," Danielle continues. "I was on the list to give interviews as I was a big advocate for Alpha—I had always been so proud to work for such a mother-friendly company. It seemed so hypocritical at the time. . . . Just as I was being interviewed by the magazine, I was having flex time taken away from me!

"Flex time has always had such inconsistency within corporations. While I had it at Alpha, I had another friend who couldn't get it. If you held a unique skill, the company was willing to do more for you. If I had been an engineer, they would have left me with me flex time. A unique skill works in your favor, flex time is so person-to-person specific."

Heather explains her rationale for remaining a part-timer despite the downsides. "Part-time work is a stopgap until the children get older. For me personally, it's a blessing. I can keep my hand in the type of job that I enjoy and still have time with my family. I have observed women who have been stay-at-home mothers for ten years trying to get back in the workforce. It takes years off where you were when you left off. Your resume shows ten years at home, a huge obstacle to overcome. And even though you can still add and subtract and have not lost your touch, it's hard to prove it to employers. I have a friend who had to go work on an assembly line when she returned to work. Now, five years later, she is a marketing manager. You are competing with those who have remained in full-time positions, which makes it even harder. The issues surrounding stay-at-home moms returning to the workplace are really there."

MOTHERS COVET PART-TIME EMPLOYMENT

"I manage four to five people on a reduced work schedule of thirty-two hours per week in a major corporation," claims Elaine, a clinical drug research manager. "Since I hold a part-time professional management position with flexible hours, I consider myself the poster child for less-than-a-full-time schedule. My hours are from 7 a.m. to 6 p.m. on Tuesdays, from 7 a.m. to 3:30 p.m. Wednesdays through Fridays, and I get Mondays off. I am lucky that my director is very family friendly. I even have a man in my department that works part-time. *But* part-timers are approved director by director; another director in my corporation says, 'Not in my group.' It depends on business needs and costs. Usually it can be done in any department—it's the director's attitude that stands in the way. Almost anything can be done on a thirty-two workweek schedule. I know—I have those hours."

Locating part-time employment takes patience and effort because part-timers are still considered unusual in today's workplace. While many part-timers are totaling up charges at the local department store counter or answering phone calls at a reception station, not everyone is able to do so. Some women are able to continue their professional careers on a part-time basis and find it rewarding. Some women, like Elaine, negotiate these positions with their current employers. Another mother, a partner in a law firm, says that the full-time mothers with young children in her legal firm are striving to become partners so that they will be able to acquire part-time hours. Others aren't as fortunate and must change jobs or start their own companies to secure the retained hours they desire. "I was happy to sacrifice income to have more time with my children," says Erica. "I gave up being a therapist to become an office manager for twenty-five hours per week with lots of flex time."

According to a survey completed by *Redbook* magazine, 61 percent of full-time employed mothers claimed they would like to work either part time or on flex-time hours.[3] In fact, 50 percent of the women interviewed started their own companies to continue working in their fields part time since that was the only way they could work on a shorter workweek schedule. Shari leads her own part-time company, teaching CPR and first aid, with the knowledge that her efforts will result in saving people's lives. Cynthia runs her own marketing consulting firm from 8 a.m. to 1 p.m. daily. Beverly is an attorney writing briefs three days per week, and Lola designs layouts for magazines as a freelance art director four days per week. None of these women envisioned themselves as entrepreneurs when they were in their early twenties. The idea of forming their own companies was a strategy to meet the goal of pursuing their careers while also caring for their children.

Katie is an example of a woman grasping an opportunity when it presented itself to her in order to secure balance in her life. "Since my church is large, it needed an emergency plan. When a vendor dropped the ball in the middle of formulating the scheme, I volunteered to complete it, as that had been my previous occupation. My fellow parishioners knew my credentials and handed the half-finished design over to me. This is how I initiated my own business. I did the research for the church's emergency plan, pulled it together, and then concluded the project. From this, I got lots of referrals, which enabled me to start up the business. I didn't even need to do much marketing. I could easily increase my business to a forty- or sixty-hour work-week, but I don't want to be on someone else's timetable or stressed out every night because I am behind schedule."

"I like having control over my hours . . . helping a sick friend with cancer, volunteering at school, socializing with my neighborhood group, and then working part-time for myself," Katie continues. "I have a great social life and enjoy the flexibility of not being tied to someone else's schedule with my job. I really enjoy life—it's true if mama is happy, then everyone is happy."

Because the part-timer bridges both worlds, she receives support from both of them as well. Part-timers declare, "When I'm in a jam, women who have been employed and are now my stay-at-home friends really help me out because they understand what I'm tackling." On the flip side, women tell of older mothers returning to work as full-time law partners and supporting part-time hours for the young mothers.

OUTLOOK FOR PART-TIMERS

Currently, many women see their innovative solutions to the male-oriented career path as a stopgap measure until they can jump back into nine-to-five "right way" job arrangement.[4] Women have been brainwashed to believe that their own resolutions are inferior to the respected full-day workweek. Some are almost apologetic in their descriptions of their part-time jobs. Confirmation of this came from several recruiters who specialize in part-time work who say that they hear women asking for part-time work "until I can get a 'real' job." Working fifteen or twenty-five hours per week as a banker or chemist or graphic designer *is* a real job! Susan Chira cites studies in *A Mother's Place: Taking the Debate about Working Mothers beyond Guilt and Blame* that shows "only a fraction of employees use these (family-friendly) benefits even when they are available because of their fear that they will be marked as less dedicated and more vulnerable to being fired."[5] Because the nature of the workforce has been structured by men's tactics and strategies, women think that if they don't dedicate forty hours per week to a career, they are not serious about their occupation.

Full-timer Ronnie claims, "It's still a male-dominated world. If I worked part time, then wanted to come back, would I be labeled as 'stepped aside'? Can my boss get over that I took time off? Could I pick up where I left off? One woman candidate that I interviewed had left her full-time job, free-lanced, and now was trying to come back. My boss was worried that she had stepped 'out of the race' and might do that again. He hesitated hiring her. Would he put that same question mark on me?"

Will these issues continue in the future? Or will part-time employment blossom? Because of the contentment and happiness I hear in the voices of part-time employed mothers and the longing to be a part-timer in the tones of many full-time workers and stay-at-home mothers' conversations, I know the desire is there. Women want to be taken seriously as an employee *and* a mother simultaneously, with time to complete both jobs well. As more and more people retain part-time positions, the professional status of the twenty- or thirty-hour workweek will become elevated.

I also believe the prospect for professional part-time jobs will become better and better over time. This will result from one major factor—industry incurring a reduction in the talent pool for hire as the population ages and retires. As baby boomers retire, all workers, including young mothers, must help to fill the vacated positions, otherwise there will be a large void in the employee population. Corporations will have to accommodate mothers' scheduling wants and needs in order to woo these mothers into the workplace and keep them there.

Industry needs women because they are 50 percent of the talent pool, and, therefore, their needs regarding career and family balance can no longer be ignored. According to the *New York Times Magazine*, "It is why the accounting firm Deloitte & Touche has more than doubled the employees on flexible work schedules over the last decade and more than quintupled the number of female partners and directors (from 97 to 567) in the same period."[6] *Time* magazine says, "at Price Waterhouse Coopers, 10 percent of the firm's female partners work on a part-time schedule."[7] Ernst and Young partner Carolyn Buck Luce says that her organization not only wants to keep working mothers but also draws those back who have left the workforce.[8]

Part-time Employment: Utmost or Dismal?

And as mentioned earlier, many mothers are not waiting for corporations to develop part-time positions; they are generating opportunities for themselves. In the first half of 2004, *Business Week* ran an article on just such women titled "The Rise of Mompreneurs," and later in the year the *Wall Street Journal* ran a front-page article titled "The Carriage Trade: Stay-at-Home Moms Get Entrepreneurial." These articles signify the rise of mothers inventing businesses to fill their personal and financial needs when no such position in corporate America currently exists for them.

And as full-time employed mothers are promoted into roles of power, they have the ability to aid other women by adopting fair part-time policies. This evolution has already started, as evidenced by Melissa, a vice president of corporate development. "As a manager of mothers who are part-timers, I often find that they work harder in three days than some other full-time employees work in five. They are trying to justify their position and are available for me to call at home on their days off with no problem. I would never hesitate in having them work for me."

Elaine, a part-time manager herself, agrees. "I think that corporations are better off to help talented women stay with them than to lose them. It's better to come up with part-time policies than to constantly retrain people. It's what I personally prefer as a manager and definitely prefer as a woman. The recent market crash took the wind out of the part-time worker sails, but with an economic upturn things might change. Priorities changed for me. . . . I was on the fast track, but I stated what hours I wanted to retain and laid out a clear plan for my employer, enabling me to spend more time with my family. I afford my employees the same flexibility, but it's a privilege, not a right."

In much the same way, high-ranking fathers in corporations married to employed wives recognize the effort their wives spend on their professional lives and, therefore, can empathize with mothers in their own corporations and set up appropriate part-time policies as well. Up until recent times, CEOs of large corporations were generally men with wives at home who had little or no sympathy for part-time working mothers or flexible scheduling.

The outlook for part-time employment is favorable over the next ten or twenty years from the corporate side based on population shifts and the early initiatives being taken by firms such as Price Waterhouse Coopers as well as from the desires of mothers. As May says, "Corporate work alone doesn't fulfill me anymore because as a full-time employed mother, I get left out of the PTA and school issues in my town. When I had young kids, I had no 'mom' friends because I needed to earn a full salary. Now I'm a part-timer so that I can be involved with the school issues."

And former stay-at-home mom Mary declares, "In my performance evaluations, I was always told what exceptional work I did. I never heard that at home, so I started my own children's portrait photography business and now get rave reviews."

It looks like part-time employment is here to stay.

NOTES

1. Cokie Roberts, *We Are Our Mothers' Daughters* (New York: William Morrow, 1998), p. 189.

2. Ann Crittenden, *The Price of Motherhood: Why the Most Important Job in the World Is Still the Least Valued* (New York: Henry Holt, 2001), p. 97.

3. Pamela Paul, "What moms want now; second-guessing your choice about whether to work or not? Join the club: Our groundbreaking survey reveals a fascinating new shift in what mothers today are really yearning for," *Redbook* (March 2003), http://www.web7.infotrac.galegroup.com/itw/infomark/591/883/52465874w7/purl=rcl_GRGM... (accessed October 15, 2004).

4. Martha N. Beck, PhD, *Breaking Point: Why Women Fall Apart and How They Can Re-Create Their Lives* (New York: Times Books, 1997), p. 372.

5. Susan Chira, *A Mother's Place: Taking the Debate about Working Mothers beyond Guilt and Blame* (New York: HarperCollins, 1998), p. 279.

6. Lisa Belkin, "The Opt Out Revolution," *New York Times*, October 26, 2003, http://www.nytimes.com/2003/10/26/magazine/26/WOMEN.html (accessed October 27, 2003).

7. Claudia Wallis, "The case for staying home: Caught between the pressures of the workplace and the demands of being a mom, more women are sticking with the kids," *Time* (March 22, 2004): 56.

8. Ibid.

SEVEN

DAYCARE—
IT CAN MAKE OR BREAK YOU

"When my children were young, childcare is what worried me most."

"**I** used a university daycare program—it was a loving, proactive, structured Montessori school, not a babysitting camp. I was never concerned about my children's well-being there, physical or emotional," declares Audrey, a Pennsylvania university professor.

If only *all* employed mothers could make the same statement. The reality of good, quality daycare is the heart of why the Wall exists—it is the crux of the issue. Caring for the children *is* the focal point of the Wall. Who will take care of them? Will the care be positive and loving? How will the children be affected by the care they receive? Some daycare options are excellent; some are just passable, while others are outright unacceptable. Obtaining reliable, loving, clean care for the children is the top concern of every mother I interviewed. It's why some mothers have always been home with their children, why numerous ones leave employment, and why others have so much guilt about careers.

Childcare can range from individual, in-home care situations to full-day childcare centers or church nurseries. In-home care includes sitters, usually mothers themselves with young children, who are willing to watch other people's children in their homes; close relatives, such as aunts and grandparents; as well as nannies who mind the children in the children's own home. Nannies can either come to the children's homes daily or live with the family. Full-day childcare centers are usually large rooms set up with various areas for playing, eating, and napping. Infants are usually accommodated in a separate room. Children come in the early part of the day as Mom and Dad go to work and leave at the close of business around 5 or 6 p.m.

DAYCARE OUT OF YOUR OWN HOME

Daycare Centers

Roughly a third of the interviewed mothers needing childcare used daycare centers in some form. Words describing daycare centers by these mothers include "loving," "clean," and "healthy." Some of them initially had a difficult time leaving their children in daycare centers, crying on their way to the office during the first few weeks of separation. Yet once the children were settled into the centers about a month later, these same mothers were so happy with daycare center accommodations that they would not move their sons and daughters to in-home care. Knowing that daycare centers are regulated and that parents are constantly dropping in unexpectedly gives numerous mothers a feeling of security that they do not obtain with in-home childcare.

According to Nancy, an attorney, "With in-home care, you really never know what is happening with your child. Are they watching television all day? Are they being spanked or being disciplined unfairly? There are no checks or balances with in-home sitters or nannies as there are with childcare centers. Using daycare by the courthouse was my first choice for Kevin, my son. I liked daycare over an in-home sitter because it was regulated. Parents were coming and going and keeping an eye on the sitters all the time. I had lunch between 10 a.m. and 2 p.m. with my son, so they never knew when I would show up. I liked that. It was my way to keep tabs on them. I continued this practice until he cried when I left. By the time I stopped seeing him at lunch, I was very comfortable with the daycare center.

"The first time I visited the daycare center, it looked like a Rumanian orphanage to me," she adds. "But both of us had to work to repay our student loans, spend for housing, and pay for food for the family. A daycare center was all that we could afford, and the first day I dropped off my son, I burst into tears. The teacher was very nice to me and handled it well. In the end, this center was great with Kevin. When I changed jobs, I also switched daycare centers so that Kevin was closer to my new location. Questionable things happened there, and I went back to the first center, even though it meant more driving. Paying for the security of Kevin, knowing that he is okay, is the best thing for him and me. I like taking him to a place where it's regulated and people are checking on it. The older he gets, the easier it gets."

Using structured, proactive teaching facilities as childcare is important to some mothers. More than one mother said to me, "I'm not looking for a babysitting camp but a school." Moms desire a provider whose daycare schedule focuses on learning, even for the youngest of children.

Laura, a hospital admittance associate, contrasts the experiences of using a teaching-focused childcare facility versus a baby-sitting focused-facility. "My children were in an excellent daycare program. Each day the provider posted a list of activities planned for the children, such as the cognitive learning activity of the day or the memory activity of the day. All of the daily activities were age appropriate whether the child was three months old or three years old. Television didn't exist in this center, a big plus as far as I was concerned. And during the summer, the children went outside in a play area and ran under the sprinkler. I received a daily sheet stating exactly what Cynthia, my daughter, did, including the learning activities as well as what she ate, when she napped, what time she was fed, and how many diapers she had. On the daily sheet, particularly for the toddlers and older children, the providers mentioned funny things that the child did that day or cute things that they might have said or that they were a little off that day.

"Even though there were three teachers in a room of twelve children, each teacher was considered a primary caregiver for four particular children, allowing for strong bonding between the teachers and children. Rollover of teachers wasn't an issue; in fact, some of the teachers had fifteen years' tenure in the center.

"The school also had a hot-meal program, where a freshly cooked lunch was delivered daily. The children sat down together as a group and ate as a family. Lunch included a meat, a vegetable, a starch, and milk. And just like at home, the kids ate what they were served, or they went hungry. Cynthia learned to drink from a cup by age one thanks to this program. In addition, the facility offered a cold breakfast, such as bagels and cream cheese, and a snack in the afternoon. All of this was included in the price."

She continues, "Parent-teacher conferences occurred quarterly, even for a six-month-old! Once a quarter, the providers offered free night symposiums on parenting techniques such as 'Redirection—Why a Better Method of Discipline.' They lasted about an hour, started at 7 p.m., and had sitters available. This whole program, from the daily learning activities to the parent-teacher conferences, was such a great daycare experience for my whole family.

"By contrast, when we changed childcare facilities because of a corporate relocation for my husband, we had an awful experience. Here, the providers never talked about what they were teaching the children; there were no specific primary-care providers assigned to the children, and there were no conferences. Lunch was not included in the price—I had to pay extra for it. And it consisted of pizza twice a week, teaching my children bad eating habits. I never heard anyone talk about 'redirection' or any parenting methods at all. I did, however, overhear the workers say, 'Oh, God, I'm so glad it's Friday. I'm so glad the day is over.' These providers were not there because they loved it, but they were there because it was a job. The teachers' attitudes reflected the high turnover. I walked in and saw the caregivers reading magazines, while the children were running circles all around them. Another time, they were playing a PG movie for the children, and Cynthia was just in kindergarten! I had never been consulted, and this was *not* okay with me.

"Cynthia came home from there crying every day, and she was only there from noon to 6 p.m. because she attended kindergarten in the morning. She was bored there and didn't want to go. It was a safe place for my daughter, but that is about it. I definitely saw it as baby-sitting, not a school. To top it off, it cost more than the previous daycare. While Cynthia was there, I managed my guilt by wearing blinders."

Mothers who have an only child or active children also like the socialization that their children obtain in daycare settings. Growing up with diversity is an advantage that daycare centers have above at-home settings with sitters or nannies. Of the women interviewed, several saw this as beneficial to their children. Laura says, "By being in daycare, Cynthia grew up with twelve brothers and sisters learning to share and get along with everyone."

Marcia, a chemical engineer, retells her childcare story. "Originally, my daughter, Elizabeth, was in someone's home until she was one. Elizabeth was so spirited that the daycare provider requested that I take her out. Now she as well as my son are both in a daycare center. My children are very social, so a daycare center is good for them. They discipline the children well. They encourage the child who was hit to say, 'You hit me, that hurts,' while the caregivers say, 'Arms are for hugging, not hitting,' helping to teach my children self-confidence. The transition from in-home care to the daycare center was hard, but the teachers are great and my children are doing well."

While most experiences with daycare centers mentioned to me were positive, I did hear of a few problems such as Laura's. Negative experiences stemmed from an individual center's issues. The mothers reporting these problems were acutely aware of this and put their children in other centers and did not switch to in-home care.

"One experience that I had with my daughter was unfortunate," says Ruth. "When she was a baby, I took her to a private daycare center in a church setting. There was one provider who adored the babies and 'loved on' them with lots of kisses. I was happy that the babies were given so much attention. But while my daughter was there, she became really sick. When I took her to the doctor, he said that she had contracted herpes. Herpes! I was, obviously, devastated. I tracked it down to the daycare worker who 'loved on' her. The woman wasn't malicious, and it wasn't intentional. She was very sweet and wonderful. I wrote a letter to the pastor and health department describing what had happened. I left that daycare center, of course, and have no idea what happened.

"After contracting herpes, my daughter always went with me wherever I worked, never attending any other childcare facility again. I did, however, have a great daycare center experience with my next child, so I am not disenchanted with daycare centers. I just had an unlucky experience."

Daycare in Another's Home

Several women used childcare in other people's houses, as a home setting with a mother or grandmotherly-type woman has great appeal. There are usually four to five children at most, and the environment is warm and loving. In addition, it has the benefit of one consistent sitter.

"Dropping my children off at one woman's home worked well for me. She took all three of my kids into her home when they were small. I would drop them off at her house on the way to the office and pick them up on the way back home after work," states Jenny, a sales director. "It was easy, it was stable. On those days when I was running a few minutes late, she would not be in a huff upon my arriving fifteen minutes late. She would have the kids all in her kitchen, where she was starting to prepare dinner. If I hadn't had that easy situation, I would never have had five children."

Physician Annette had a different experience. "My first daycare was in a private home, a great situation, with one other child. I had no worries, and if I had a slow day, I could pick her up early. But with two children, it became more of a struggle. The home setting was structured, and I had to leave at 5 p.m. to get my children, or the daycare would charge me for being late. With two children, that can add up! And then my partners in the practice looked down on me for leaving promptly every day. Because of this situation, my neighbors helped by picking up my children from daycare when I was unable to leave on time."

Talking with Carly, a woman who ran a childcare business from her home for five years, I saw how much love caregivers can bestow onto their little clients. "I had my own childcare business for children under age two. Many facilities would not take children that age, so I always had clients. The most important factor was that the families had to like my lifestyle, as their children were in my home. Some families treated me as a mentor, a friend, or an adviser. Only one parent treated me as hired help. Even though this was *my* business, I was willing to work with the parents . . . and that was the key to my success. Examples of working with parents include 'no disposable diapers' to breast feeding. One mother wanted 'no disposables,' and I told her that it was fine, but I would not rinse them. She agreed to my stipulation of taking them home each night. Another mother came and nursed her child every afternoon. As the baby grew older, she wanted to leave with her mother when the mother was returning to the office. I stepped in and asked the mother to pump her milk and send it in to avoid upsetting her daughter in the afternoons. The mother agreed to my request."

Carly adds, "The babies came with me whenever I drove my own children to and from elementary school. There were times that I had five baby seats in my car at once. When I went into school to see programs that included my children, I always had two or three babies with me. These babies were exposed to good things that many infants do not get to see. I didn't take them shopping unless I absolutely had to. Some people were fine with it; others were reluctant. Many loved it, really liked their kids being out and about. Others were pleased that their infants were getting interaction with other babies. I baby-sat from four to six children at a time. Once in a while, I had five infants. The babies loved it! The youngest child I ever had was two weeks old. Since she came to us at such a young age, she became part of our family's life. She was the only child I kept past the age of two."

RELATIVES PROVIDING CHILDCARE

"My mother was a stay-at-home mom, and I remember how nice it was to see her when I came home from high school," says Susan, an accountant. "I can't be there for my children because of my job, but my father meets the boys every day after school when they come in the door. Luckily, my parents are also my neighbors, so they are there daily for the boys after classes and for emergencies. I come home shortly after the school bus arrives with my sons."

Approximately one-third of the mothers interviewed have either their husbands or relatives watch their children while they are at the workplace. Mothers consider it a blessing to have their parents or in-laws as the baby-sitter. Who better to raise the children than those with years of experience? Those who have their husbands watching the kids are also extremely grateful.

"My children were in a daycare center in town, but now my husband is the primary caregiver," says Ronnie, director of procurement. "He is currently working from home, and it's clearly better for the children. Now he puts the kids on the bus, and they can have play dates like the other children on the street, no more running back and forth from the daycare center. The days were so rushed before. . . . There was no downtime, no playtime. Now we can linger in bed, take our time getting dressed, and eat breakfast at home in the mornings. The children can come home on the school bus, have a snack, play with the kids on the street, and still have time for homework in the evenings. The kids are talking a lot more than they did before, maybe because the stress factor is lower, maybe it's because there is simply more time to talk. My job is under my control, so I can take time off if necessary. I also have my mother-in-law down the road who is willing to help out in emergency situations. Things are running smoothly right now."

Audrey has an unusual story. "Since I waited to have a baby until I was older, my grandparents kept asking me when I was going to have a child. I answered by saying that I wouldn't have a child until they moved close to me. Now at the time, I lived in Maryland, and they lived in Vermont. They called my bluff and moved to my town in Maryland! I then had a son, and my grandparents took care of him for the first five years of his life while I worked. I dropped him off at their house in the morning, and my husband would pick him up in the late afternoon. I was so blessed! My husband worked at night. He left as I drove up to our house, so I was never with him. But my son saw him as he rotated through all of the family members throughout the day. We tried to have a 'normal' family life, but it was hard because we were seldom together. We didn't eat dinner together and usually were never all together at the same time. Yet the unusual situation with my grandparents gave my son a great sense of family."

And for Alison, help came from several family members over time. "When I had my oldest son, Sam, I was living with my mother, so I paid her to take care of my son while I went to the office, until he was three. It was the best possible solution for me. But when I moved out, my mother simultaneously started to work herself, so I had to enroll Sam in daycare. I was never happy with the daycare facilities, and I switched him several times. It was so hard, after having had a relative who loved him, taking care of him, and then going to a center where the teachers had no feelings for the children. They did not care what Sam did as long as he did not disrupt the class. . . . They did not care what he ate—or even if he ate at all. It was not a nice feeling. At age four, he went to prekindergarten school, and that was much better." Alison continues, "With my second son, Alex, my husband worked nights, and I worked days. In addition, my sister-in-law lived with us. So between all of these schedules and adults coming and going, my children were taken care of. It wasn't a perfect arrangement, but it worked out. When my husband's schedule changed, Alex had to go to daycare, while Sam went to school. But by that time, I found a much better daycare center in a church."

Alison adds, "Each summer we had different arrangements. Some summers we had outside sitters come in; other summers my boys went to the grandparents' homes. Other relatives also helped us out, sisters and sisters-in-law. I know that I had a unique situation where so many family members helped us out, but it worked. We were lucky that we never had to put more than one child in daycare at a time because it is so expensive. I don't know what we would have done without family as I don't think that we could have afforded both boys in daycare at once."

DAYCARE IN YOUR OWN HOME

"My children have always had a sitter who could drive them whenever and wherever necessary at my home," claims Sharon from Washington. "I had an au pair from France baby-sit for two years when the children were young. And as the children grew, I had a college-age girl for several years. Using young girls in their late teens or early twenties with lots of energy to watch the boys after school has been key. I have used an agency to find people, put up want ads in local colleges, and received word-of-mouth recommendations from sitters when they had to leave. I rolled over several nannies that way, and it worked out well for me. I need them only from 3:15 to 5:30 p.m. now. I'm always home by 5:30 p.m. and work just thirty minutes from home, which is good in case of emergencies."

The convenience and comfort of having someone care for your children in your our home is a big plus for numerous mothers. Having children play with their own toys in their own home; watching only approved television shows, if they watch television at all; as well as being able to direct exactly what food the children are allowed to eat are great comforts for some mothers. This may sound perfect to those who have never had the opportunity to leave their children at home, yet as all options, it has its negative aspects. In fact, the *Wall Street Journal* reported that 15 to 20 percent of au pair placements don't work out because of bad fits, as a result of everything from personality clashes to homesickness.[1]

Mothers like Jo Ellen, a recruiter, who have hired live-in au pairs reveal that it is much like having a teenager constantly in your home, even though your children are still young. "My children went to KinderCare from babies to age five and then had a new au pair each year for the next six years. I actually had nine au pairs live with my family over that timeframe, but three were there for a very short period of time. I knew within weeks when they were unacceptable and immediately switched for another one whenever that was necessary. It was an adequate situation using au pairs, but not great. The problems were typical of having an older teenager in your home: boyfriend problems, not wanting you to set out rules yet wanting to drive the car, using the telephone. My au pairs drove my car with my kids in it but did not want any parameters! That did not fly with me. My au pairs had the objective of learning English and then going home after a year when they came to this country. After six years of this, I cut a deal with my employer to leave at 4 p.m. so that I needed no sitters. My oldest came into an empty house alone, and I reached home a few minutes later, just before his brother walked in the door. I must admit, I got stuck a few times and could not make it home for an hour or so, but I just got tired of having someone else in my house."

The only reason that some mothers have the ability to continue their vocations is the continuity of daycare that they have found for their children. Several mothers claim that they can maintain their careers only because they have either the constant presence of one nanny or consistent childcare providers over several years. Doris's is one story of working through compromises in order to maintain acceptable daycare that meets her scheduling needs.

"We initially wanted a nanny and had a parade of sitters go through the house until we found one in her twenties that we liked. We kept her for a couple of years by overpaying her. She drove to and from our home daily, which was convenient for me. When we had the second child, she could not handle both of the children at once, so we had to change sitters. It was at this point that I found the nanny from heaven. She was fast, efficient, and a conscientious person in her fifties, a grandmotherly type. Unfortunately, she could not handle my second son, John, as an infant along with my three-year-old son, Sean, so I sent Sean to daycare. The nanny took Sean to the childcare facility and brought him home again. He did not like this particular nanny, but she was great to John. In fact, the rest of the family liked her so much that she practically became a member of our family. We have actually flown out to visit her. John still loves her to this day. We always gave her everything she wanted, and she left only because her husband had to move. Both of the boys then went to daycare when the nanny left, as John was two and Sean was five. Between the switch of going from a grandmotherly nanny who spoiled him to a daycare center that constantly was changing teachers, John was traumatized. So I switched both children to a Montessori school where everyone was happier."

Doris continues her story. "Because I leave at 6 a.m. to go exercise and reach work by 8 a.m., we needed a babysitter to get the boys ready for school and drop them off as well as pick them up after school. We found a young woman in her twenties, Cheyenne, who was flexible and willing to work our hours. Since my husband leaves later in the morning, the sitter came in at 7 a.m., fed John and Sean breakfast, got them dressed, and drove them to school. Later in the day, she picked them up at school, gave them a snack, took them to their different after-school activities, and saw that their homework got done. We paid her $10.50 per hour and guaranteed her a thirty-five-hour workweek. Since Cheyenne was not ambitious, she was happy with this arrangement because she could afford her own apartment on those wages. We bought her a cell phone so that we could get in contact with her at any time. In addition, we gave Cheyenne a credit card so that she could buy items for the children as well as gas for her car. We made it as easy as possible for her to work for us."

"She was, however, a difficult sitter," Doris adds. "Cheyenne had trouble being on time and let the boys watch a lot of television. She was more like a teenager than an adult. But we tolerated her because she was so flexible and worked whatever hours we threw at her. We paid her enough so that we were her only source of income, and we treated her well, as one of our pet peeves is those who treat nannies badly.

"Even though Cheyenne had been with us for a long time, we got exasperated with her. She had a problem with being on time. She was late picking Sean up from school, and she was late getting to our house in the morning. Sean has ADD and must get his medicine one hour prior to school starting. If she was late getting to my house in the morning, my son didn't get his medicine when he needed it. My husband had to set the clock to remind himself to give my son the medicine to compensate for the nanny being late. Cheyenne also quarreled with Sean a lot. My son makes nannies cry because he does not want anyone to watch him but me. Let's face it, he's just a hyperactive eight-year-old and not easy to deal with. He has a tough behavioral plan that must be followed. We didn't always get what we paid for from Cheyenne, but she was very flexible. Her mantra was 'no problem.' She was the backup when my kids were sick, would baby-sit at night, and stayed as late as we needed her during the week."

Doris concludes, "Unfortunately, we finally had to let her go because of her continual difficult time in following our rules. Now we use a 'village' of other parents as well as my own parents to coordinate elaborate carpooling schedules, particularly in the summer when school is out and day camp programs run from 10 a.m. to 3 p.m., making it quite complicated for employed parents. It is the cooperative, congenial parents in my neighborhood that help make employment and parenthood a mutual success."

Edith is another woman who has tried a variety of daycare options and found that all of them involve compromises. "I have had a sitter come into my home daily during the week, have had live-in au pairs, and am currently taking my youngest daughter to a woman's house. Having someone in my home with the kids is best because they can still be in their pajamas when I leave and don't have to rush in the mornings. The au pairs helped with the laundry but did not cook at all, had two accidents with our car, and brought male visitors in the house who burned our carpets with their cigarettes. There are pluses and minuses with all the different types of daycare. I rush to get home for the ones who drive to my house so they can get home, but they will shop for food and start dinner for me. Now, of course, I grocery shop, prepare dinner, get my daughter ready in the morning, drop her off at the sitter's home, and then pick her up again, I do it all! For me, it's best having someone in the house because at least some of the household chores are handled."

THE WALL BETWEEN WOMEN

Like some mothers, Mary had an ideal childcare situation until she was forced to move. Her current method of childcare in her new town is not as effective as her previous daycare was. "When I was working and my children were young, everyone loved my nanny. Neighbors and friends took my kids everywhere with them so that my nanny would come and help out. Sometimes they dumped their kids at my house, knowing that my nanny was there to watch all of them. This may sound offensive, but I liked it because it kept me connected with the neighbors and their children when I wasn't home much. Then I moved to another town and was forced to hire another sitter. My children weren't invited places because the moms in the new town wanted other stay-at-home mothers to interact with, and I was at the office. I had a few young nannies that were not terrific. Frankly, I would have been better off sending my children to daycare or hiring an older woman."

For mothers running their office from home, the most difficult option is watching the children themselves. They gain some relief by sending the kids to preschool a few days per week, but that covers only eight or nine hours out of a forty-hour workweek. Five percent of the employed women that I interviewed used this option. Lack of available daycare or childcare costs forced them into this situation.

"My daughter, Emma, goes to preschool three days per week and is home the rest of the time," says Calle, an office manager for an Internet company. "It helps that Emma is older and more self-sufficient than most two-year-olds. But it is burdensome if I am conducting business on the phone, and she falls and hurts herself. Emma knows the difference between the work phone and the home phone. It makes her independent . . . too independent, I am afraid. I worry that I push her aside because of work."

PART-TIME CHILDCARE

While full-time daycare is available in-home and at childcare facilities across the country, part-time daycare varies regionally. For mothers in the Northeast, it's arduous and sometimes next to impossible to find. Daycare centers usually want and can get full-time clients. A slot filled by a child attending part time could be filled by a full-time patron in this competitive marketplace. Finding a part-time sitter is expensive, if you are lucky enough to even locate one. Throughout the South, however, there are part-time options, with

Mother's Day Out in church nurseries. And, according to women interviewed, the West is supportive of part-time working mothers and has suitable daycare options to match.

"I love Mother's Day Out," says Shari, a part-time CPR trainer. "It is three to four hours per week once or twice a week in a church school nursery. It is very inexpensive and gives moms about six to eight hours per week to either get errands done without children, work part time, or just socialize as an adult. It usually runs from 9 a.m. to 2 p.m. Run by grandmotherly types, it's like going to a play group. The fee is quite low, but you do have to enroll. For a while, it was a drop-off system, but then they evolved to having you sign up for particular days of the week so that they have enough teachers to meet state guidelines for the teacher-to-children ratios. If a child is sick, you still pay. But no one complains because everyone is grateful that it's available. Some centers have drop-in daycare for at-home mothers on an as-needed basis. If the room is full, however, the drop-in children can't stay. Therefore, mothers who really require those eight hours of childcare every week, sign up for it religiously."

Another mother, Charlene, was also grateful for Mother's Day Out. "During the first year of my son's life, I took him to the office with me. When I worked in a church atmosphere on a part-time basis, my office was at the opposite end of the campus from the rest of the staff so that, as a baby, my son Austin was far away from the other employees. I was very lucky because I had a large office and could take the playpen and swing with me. Then he went to Mother's Day Out three days a week after he started to walk. It cost me approximately $8 per day. They had licensed, certified daycare providers and took children ranging from birth to age five. This program was subsidized by the Christian education program of the church where it was held. The church saw this as support for the community at large and, therefore, did not teach religion to the children while they were there. Mother's Day Out was what made part-time work even possible for me. It was an absolute blessing. I could not have afforded to pay the rates at other daycare facilities. Without Mother's Day Out and the tax credits for daycare, I couldn't have worked part time.

"And I loved what I did, planning and playing five services of music for fifteen hundred parishioners. I also couldn't have done this without my husband's help. He watched the children on weekends and nights when I had to perform. My son went to Mother's Day Out for five days per week when I was sick with my second pregnancy and was confined to bed rest. When my daughter, Brooke, was born, she was medically difficult and slept only nine minutes at a time. Brooke was expelled from Mother's Day Out after only two days. They couldn't handle her, as she needed the uprightness and pressure of a snuggly almost constantly. She screamed almost nonstop for those first nine months. After that, I found a grandmotherly-type sitter who watched her until she was fifteen months old. At that point, medicine improved her temperament, and Brooke could go back to Mother's Day Out."

Erica, a part-time office manager, primarily uses her family to cover her childcare needs. "Since I work part-time, I can usually arrange my hours around the children being in school or my husband being at home. I teach several full-day seminars on office management during the year when I have to hire a grandparent-type couple who charge quite a bit. I give them my seminar schedule for the whole year and get them to commit to the dates. If they are sick, it is a disaster, as I have twenty-five students waiting for me to teach a class. I try not to commit to these full-day kind of events unless I must."

Lola claims, "As a part-time employed mother, I bought the number of days per week that I needed from a childcare facility. Oregon is supportive of part-time working moms, and Portland has lots of options like this. In the Northeast, the career and structure is more important, but here in the Northwest, it's very laid back. We wear jeans and bring our kids to the office. We have all seen each others' kids in the workplace. This part-time experience gave me confidence as a parent."

WHAT'S BEST?

Numerous conflicting studies have been conducted over what is better for the child, Mom or daycare? One study concludes that Mom is better at raising her own children, while another claims daycare is equivalent. Yet another resolves that daycare is actually better than Mom because of daycare's bolstering of self-confidence. The studies have, however, reached consensus on the fact that mothers who handle their sons and daughters with sensitivity have more secure children. They also agree that children whose mothers handle them with insensitivity or those who change childcare more than once a year are more insecure.[2] This seems to say that daycare is not a problem if someone is listening to the kids at home.

According to Ellen Galinsky, president of the Families and Work Institute, the problem lies not with employment itself but with *how* mothers work. Galinsky conducted a survey with over a thousand children, ages eight to eighteen, to determine how they feel about employed parents. The responses reveal that the children didn't desire more time with their parents, but they did express wishes that their parents were less stressed and tired at the end of the workday. From this, Galinsky concludes that mothers' jobs aren't the issue, but their fulfillment at work affecting their mood and energy at the end of the day is. If they are satisfied at work, they can be more attentive and energetic with their sons and daughters at home.[3]

NOTES

1. Sue Shellenbarger, "Number of Au Pairs Increases Sharply as Rule Change Allows Longer Stays," *Wall Street Journal* (February 10, 2005): D1.

2. Sheila Kitzinger, *Ourselves as Mothers: The Universal Experience of Motherhood* (New York: Addison-Wesley, 1995), p. 10.

3. Leora Tanebaum, *Catfight: Women and Competition* (New York: Seven Stories Press, 2002), p. 261.

EIGHT

SHIFTING LIFESTYLES

"When all is said and done and the children are grown, you can't go back and do it all over again. You want to do it right the first time."

So how *do* women determine what to do? How do they *decide*? How do they *choose*? Almost all women are employed prior to having children, so when do they decide to continue employment or to stay home? Initially, the majority of women continue to work after childbirth.[1] Then, over the next few months or years, numerous mothers begin to feel inordinately exhausted and worn down—or realize that childhood cannot be put on the back burner but a career can—or decide that they are tired of never seeing their husbands anywhere except in bed sleeping. This happens to such a degree that they consider turning in their occupational nametags to become mothers on a full-time basis.

Women begin reviewing their finances to determine if they can afford this luxury in today's economic environment. Can they continue their career in a scaled-down level? Can they still pay the rent or mortgage? What kind of car will the family be able to drive? How often will the family be able to eat out, if at all? Will the family have to eat macaroni and cheese for the next few years until their spouses receive substantial pay increases? Then the crucial decision is made.

Ronnie, a director of procurement, reveals, "Going up the ladder, I will need to be more available as the demands will be tenfold, and it will be harder and harder to disconnect from the office. Talking with my boss during my review, I told him that I want to be a vice president over the next several years. His reply was, 'Okay, if this is what you want, you must be available 24/7.' I consider that as being married to your job, and I already do that. Over the next few years, I will have a big decision to make. I'm the first woman in procurement to get to where I am. If I leave, will that set other women in the department back?"

In *Maternal Desire*, Daphne de Marneffe describes Ronnie's inclinations, not as duties or necessities or biological imperatives but as a raw desire to raise her

133

own children. She claims that feminism has championed women's choices but has neglected to acknowledge a mother's desire to simply care for her own children.[2] So women are inevitably torn between fulfilling careers and loving children at home, giving them a continual feeling of internal conflict.

FROM WORKPLACE TO HOME

Some mothers either briefly consider staying home, but then toss the idea aside quickly because of monetary issues, or do not contemplate it at all because they enjoy their current positions within the workplace. Some fear if they resign, they will never be hired again. Others think long and hard to reach their conclusions on feasible next steps. Over half of the mothers who drop out of the workforce do so when their children are between the ages of a few weeks and five years old because they aren't pleased with the daily trade-offs that they incur between employment and family.[3] Many mothers are usually pushed to the breaking point before they consider leaving the office and staying home. In order to quit, one mother I interviewed went to a psychiatrist to help her make her choice. She says, "It was a big decision. I was so nervous and uptight, I had to take tranquilizers."

So many moms have similar stories that when I retell them, I had to double-check that I was not writing up the same person's story twice! Here are Pamela's, Tracy's, and Sara's similar stories of resigning from work.

"Acting as a single mother in a two-parent home, I felt isolated from both the employed mothers with vocations *and* the stay-at-home moms," says Pamela. "My husband was gone from 7 a.m. to 7 p.m., leaving all the childcare totally up to me. Since I had my own job, I had no interaction with either employed mothers or stay-at-home moms unless they were co-workers because of the lack of hours in the day. I had time for no one except my children, not even my husband. In the end, I couldn't do it all, and that is why I left work."

"When I was working full time, the only other mothers that I knew were my sisters and sister-in-law, who were both at-home moms. They pitied me," claims Tracy. "They clearly wondered how I got everything done. I just did it . . . working, laundry, cleaning. My husband traveled a lot, so I felt as if I was a single mother. I took the kids to school, ran errands at lunch, grocery shopped after work, made dinner, bathed the kids, and collapsed."

Sara concurs. "When I was at the bank, I was just surviving, not living. Each morning I woke the children, fed and dressed them, dropped them off at daycare, went to work, bought the groceries on the way home from work, came home, made dinner, bathed the children, and then crawled into bed. Examining the cost of daycare, clothes, carryout dinners, and taxes, I realized that I was bringing home almost no income. The dollar figure was so small considering the stress and exhaustion, it was a slap in the face."

For some women, like Mary Ann and Holly, the decision is easy and straightforward, but the shift itself takes adjustment. For others, like Diane, it was a difficult choice.

"When I first stayed home after being a physician, I felt like a fish out of water. It's a different world," declares Mary Ann. "My husband, also a doctor, and I transferred cities and moved into an executive development with big, pricey homes. While I was looking to purchase my home, everyone thought that I was the doctor's *wife*. No one knew that *I* was a physician, too. The real estate lady proudly said to me, 'We have ten Hobby Lobby stores here.' I had absolutely no idea what she was talking about. Later, I learned that it is the Home Depot of arts and crafts stores, something that the real estate agent assumed every Southern mother at home is avidly seeking out."

Mary Ann continues, "Lacking in social graces, feeling deficient in at-home skills, and caring for a young family, I perceived that the other mothers in my neighborhood were experts at raising families, making me feel awkward. I went on a playdate with the ladies in the big, expensive houses. They had all brought nice lunches for their children—little sandwiches, box drinks or bottles, and fruit. I had brought nothing, having no idea that this was the protocol, that lunch would be involved. I scrounged around in the bottom of my diaper bag to grab something for my son. I came up with some beef jerky. I felt bad that I had not brought his lunch, but I'm learning.

"I am mastering the lingo and social dances—joining church groups, fussing in the kitchen, bemoaning that our homes are a mess. I *am* learning to hold my own. Now, I welcome the new neighbors, have joined a reading group at church, and even bake for funerals. I have become a 'church lady.' Ten years ago, I never thought that this would happen. I am glad that I am not ashamed to say that I am a stay-at-home mother, yet it will take years to know who 'I' am."

Holly laboriously adopted home life not because she wanted to fit in with the other stay-at-home mothers, like Mary Ann did, but because her relationship with her husband changed. "My difficulty in adjusting to staying home was in regard to handing over command of the household. I had been the head of household for nine years as a single mother. Having had my children out of wedlock, I had been the head of everything for a long time. Never having lived with another adult before I married, there were many adjustments. Now I was sharing—it was hard learning to share. We pooled our resources, and I handed over command of the finances. It was hard to be second in command, to be the housekeeping staff, and to have no income. I missed earning my own money, as income is power. I wanted to work so that I did not have to ask for $50 if I wanted to buy something silly. I did not want to have to justify my purchases. It was not a matter of staying within my means—I feel emasculated with no income."

"We had been equal while dating as I had been a documentation manager," Holly continues. "Then, when I lost my job after we were married, I felt like he became my dad. I had to clear everything with him. My husband even did the grocery shopping, he totally controlled the money. This was just too much for me! I needed emotional support, so I looked to the other stay-at-home mothers in the neighborhood for friendship.

"Unfortunately, they were bitchy when referring to their husbands. According to these mothers in my neighborhood, as soon as the woman stops working, the respect from the spouse goes down. That did not help my outlook; in fact, it was bad for my marriage. In addition, they scheduled nickel-and-dime activities that really added up after a while. It became a big source of strife for us. He had promised to give me $100 per month for myself, and I counted on getting that money to participate in the 'mommy' activities. Sometimes he did not give me the money, causing me to feel disappointed because I had to miss out on some of the women's plans. He was smothering me.

"When I asked for babysitting money, he wanted to know why I needed a sitter. I explained that I just wanted a few hours a week for myself. So I left him with the kids on a Saturday. He said that it wasn't so bad to take care of them all day. Sure, he gave them a three-hour nap, didn't make dinner, didn't bathe the kids, and the place was a mess when I got home. His standards for caring for the children weren't the same as what he expected out of me. On Saturdays, my husband went golfing, while I was doing the same work Monday through Sunday. I had to stand up for myself. So I went on strike for a few weeks, forcing him to see what I did every day and rapidly gaining his appreciation. Now I use Mother's Day Out for a few hours on Tuesdays and Thursdays, so I have some time for myself.

"He was controlling and not treating me as an adult. I realized that I was letting him do this to me, so I explained this to him. Luckily, it was a bloodless coup. We came to a mutual agreement. He now puts money into an account for me from which I pay for half the groceries, half the sitting, the medical expenses, and the kids' clothes. Before this, when the kids needed shoes, I always had to ask for money. I never felt as though I was a parent in the household. There is also an amount of money earmarked for me in there as well. It's my money, used for things like lunching with the ladies, that he cannot take back. Since we have had the discussion, he is treating me the way he did when we were dating, as an equal."

Some women, like Diane, don't want to resign. They love their careers along with the power and status that accompany their jobs. Leaving comes only at the end of a struggle of trying to care for the children while also maintaining a high level of professionalism in the workplace.

"Having the second child is what did it for me," states Diane, a former sales representative of medical supplies. "I always felt that I had to work. For the first eighteen months of my daughter's life, we used in-home daycare with two different sitters. The second nanny had a playmate for my daughter, as she had a child the same age as my daughter. I really liked the socialization that my daughter was getting in her home. Since my job demanded going into surgery to assist in the usage of my products on occasion, it was perfect dropping my daughter off at the nanny's home early, 6 a.m. or 7 a.m., to be on time for the various surgical procedures.

"Then, when my daughter turned eighteen months old, I started taking her to daycare. Because the center opened early, I could take her either at 7 a.m. or 8:30 a.m., depending on my selling schedule for the day, so the change in childcare arrangements did not affect my client relationships. My daughter loved the childcare center and really thrived, but I still cried when I left her there. I kept her with me as much as I could and did my paperwork at night after she was asleep. And even though I was with her and played with her quite a bit, my mind was always on work, so I feel as though I lost a lot of time with her. With my sales job, I could not just turn it off at the door. While I sat on the floor and played with her, I was thinking about how I could have made the last presentation better or how I was going to approach tomorrow's client. I personally did not handle being a mother and holding a

THE WALL BETWEEN WOMEN

professional job well. I did not give my child 100 percent, as I was thinking about either the last sale pitch or the next surgical procedure.

"When I had my son, my mother came to live with us for a while to help me get adjusted to working and having two children. Now my daughter went to preschool three days per week but otherwise was home with my mother and son. There were days that my mother rode with me in the car while I was making sales calls so that I could breastfeed my son. Other days she would stay home with the baby. It was chaotic. I hired a nanny to help me out once my mother left. Physically, it was crazy. One day I said to myself, 'What am I trying to prove?' I didn't want to be unfair to my customers or my children or my husband and felt that I was being that way to everyone! So I stopped. Once I quit, I said to myself, 'Why didn't I do this before?' Life was so much simpler then.

"I was vacillating if I should continue working or not with my first child and sort of knew that the end was coming when the second child was on the way," Diane continues. "I never did find the right person to take care of the baby and drive the three-year-old to and from school, so that helped me to make my decision to stop. When I was selling, life was about getting through it. I was employed my whole life, through high school, through college. I had a strong work ethic, and it made sense to me to continue with my career. My mother was a teacher with three children and did lots of volunteer work. But then my father was home a lot to help her. My husband, on the other hand, was traveling quite a bit and couldn't help me with the kids. When I had to travel a whole week to call on distant accounts, we would have to coordinate who could be home for the children. There were times that I had to fly to the corporate headquarters in New York and stop along the way in Indiana to drop off the children with my mother and then stop again on the way home to pick them up on the way back to South Carolina. I can't think how many times I had to make those airport pit stops. I did make it working six months with two children. I loved my job, but it was the right decision to stop. Looking back, I should have resigned earlier. If I could do it over again, I wouldn't have continued selling. I felt as if I never had my daughter 100 percent; I was sharing her with my job. Some careers you can walk away from at the end of each day and focus on the family at night, but not mine."

A few mothers are almost pushed out of the workplace because of continually moving either around the United States or even out of the country for their spouse's career. It is difficult for a woman to maintain a solid employment track record if her husband is being transferred every two years. In addition, many women in this situation either stop working out of the home or take up part-time employment specifically to be the consistent caregiver for their children amid all the other fluctuations in their lives.

SCALING BACK ON EMPLOYMENT

Then there are women like Hope who scale back their employment rather than stop altogether to improve the family situation. They love their careers, independence, and identity, but they abhor the turmoil in their homes. The reduction in hours enables these mothers to continue a career, albeit at a slower pace, while also interacting with their children more during the week at home.

"When I had my daughter, I was a director of human resources in a Fortune 100 company, and my husband was president of his corporate division," says Hope. "We were a corporate couple, having little or no interaction with other young families up to this point. My entire life had included employment, with maternity leave being the first time I was given permission to stop and rest. My initial plans comprised having peace and quiet with my new baby, Heather, over my eight-week maternity leave. When I came home from the hospital with my infant daughter, I had no rest or quiet as planned because my condominium was in the midst of redecoration. I was constantly directing the project. After three weeks of being at home, the office started to call, and I just gave up, returning to the workplace after five weeks, not the planned eight. The nanny came in the door, and I revolved out with my briefcase the fifth week after Heather was born. I lost that early time with my daughter, and I will regret it for the rest of my life.

"Since my husband wanted a live-in nanny, we initially hired a nineteen-year-old from Europe. We clearly explained to her that we would need extra help on weekends as my husband's position demanded a high level of socializing. I also traveled and occasionally had night meetings, so she needed to be available during her off hours for babysitting. She would be well compensated for the extra time. A car was provided since running small errands such as obtaining groceries was part of the nanny's job. When I walked in the door from work, the nanny handed me the baby and was out the door, socializing with her new friends. After seven months, she quit, giving me one week's notice because she said she was working too hard and wanted her weekends free. I panicked since I knew no teenagers in the neighborhood, knew none of the stay-at-home mothers, and had no family living close to me. In essence, I had no support system. Even my husband was no help, as he focused 100 percent on his job and related travels, wanting nothing to do with childcare.

"While searching for another nanny through agencies, one from within the country this time, I worked from home as much as possible and took Heather to the office when necessary. Finally, I hired a sitter who lived in during the week and went home on weekends. The holidays rolled around about two months after she had started baby-sitting for us. We gave her a turkey and a bottle of wine as a gift. The Monday after the holidays, I waited and waited for her to return, but she never came back. I tried to contact her and couldn't—she just vanished. She could have disappeared with my baby! Now I was terrified about finding a new sitter. I had no relatives, no support, no help from my husband. Everything fell to me.

"I found a grandmotherly-type nanny who agreed to stay one month because of my emergency situation. When I checked her out, I asked if she had a police record. I was so worried, but I had no choice—I was desperate for help. While I was lucky to find her, I had to drive one hour to pick her up on Sunday night and then drive back home one hour with Heather in the car. Then, on Friday night, I had the reverse, driving one hour with the baby in the car to drop her off, taking an additional hour to return home again. My husband refused to help with my daughter during these drives. You play the cards you are dealt the best you can . . . do the best at your job, be the best wife, be the best mother.

"After three months of searching—the grandmotherly nanny had agreed to sit for me two months longer than planned—I found a permanent nanny," Hope continues. "At this point, Heather was eleven months old and already on her third nanny. Fortunately, this nanny met all our needs and stayed for her full-year assignment. At the end of her year, I started yet another 'nanny search.' During this quest, my husband's parents came to help out with Heather, and I once again worked from home. I had no time for myself or my husband, and I was always behind on everything. After three weeks, I successfully found another nanny. But now my daughter could talk and cried every morning, 'Please do not leave me, Mommy.' I cried all the way to work. When I returned home in the evenings, Heather was always hyper. All she wanted to do was play with her father and me. My husband and I could not even carry on a conversation.

"After the nanny had been with us for two years, we took a three-day vacation, dropping the nanny and Heather off at the grandparents' house on the way out. When we returned, my mother-in-law claimed that the nanny had slapped my daughter. The nanny as well as Heather denied it, yet I still was in a panic when I went to work now. I was always wondering what was happening to my child while I was away.

"So I moved on to nanny number six, who was great. She had been there three months when she had a nervous breakdown from boyfriend problems. We helped her through her breakdown, letting her take two months off. Just as we were expecting her to return, she decided to start another career, leaving me yet again without a sitter. By age five, my daughter was on nanny number seven. At this point, I was telling my bosses that I could not manage working five days per week. I wanted to resign because of daycare issues, to be a better wife and better mother. I wanted to switch priorities because I could not do it all and felt unappreciated by everyone. Yet my husband encouraged me to keep working, so I remained employed. It was like walking in quicksand—where would I step into it? Where would everything be okay?

"One day I came home from work early to take Heather to the doctor. We were going to the pool after the doctor's appointment, so I invited nanny number seven to join us. She said she had other plans and turned us down. When I came home after the pool, I listened to a message on my answering machine saying that a friend hoped that I was all right and that if I needed any help, since my nanny resigned, to please call. Immediately I ran upstairs to see that the nanny had vacated while I was out. She had given me no notice and let me know she was quitting by just leaving a note in her room. I was shocked, surprised, and totally baffled. The hardest part was telling my daughter that the nanny needed to go away. Puckering up her lips, she started to cry and pushed her nose against the glass and said, 'She loves me and will come back.' Falling on my knees, I broke down and cried, saying, 'I am done!' For the rest of the day, I was running in and out of the bathroom, throwing up from being so upset. I felt as if I was coming from a place of total destruction and failing on all fronts. I decided then and there I would never have another nanny.

"When I told my boss that I was quitting, he asked, 'What can we do to keep you?' I answered, 'It's time I made a life decision.' Agreeing to work only sixteen hours per week while my child was in school, I stepped down from my high-level, management position. Managing my own schedule, consulting from my kitchen table, traveling only when Heather can join me, that is what works best for me." Hope concludes, "I will always wonder when my daughter is having emotional issues if I could have prevented it by raising her differently in her younger years."

RETURNING TO THE WORKPLACE

Reestablishing oneself with either a part-time or full-time career is done by many but can be emotionally daunting for some. A partner in a part-time recruiting firm, Donna told me that "stay-at-home mothers think that they are ready to return to the office. They get their resume together and bone up on their interview skills. But the real test is when they are called for a job assignment. If they are prepared emotionally and mentally, they go all out for the interview. But if they say, 'It is too far' or 'I have to be home for the bus,' those are the women who aren't really ready for employment yet."

Pamela is one of those mothers who is intellectually yearning to reenter her career but not emotionally ready. "I had a master plan to return to the office on a part-time basis. My old boss welcomed me with open arms and said that he would certainly consider part-time work. The nanny who I know well from next door would come over for four days a week from 9:30 a.m. to 3 p.m. when her other charges were at school. That would give me twenty-two hours per week for business, without counting night work that could be completed after the children went to bed. It sounds so good, having a nanny you know to take care of your children, working until 3 p.m., but it is not realistic for what I do.

"Ultimately, I will go back, but I still want to be here when my daughter gets off of the bus at noon," Pamela continues. "I want to see her as soon as she comes home from school. Once she goes to school until 4 p.m., I will consider going back to my old career. But then I have my two-year-old son to consider—I do not want to put him in daycare. It is so hard to go back as I would start all over again with no accounts, basically starting at ground zero. After calculating the numbers, I determined the first two-thirds of my income after tax would go to the sitter. If I did well, I would be left with $10,000 after a year of working four days 9 a.m. to 3 p.m. Once I was working a year or so, I would increase my income. But the economy is not great. Once the economy is better, maybe I will go back. Many people say the young years are important for bonding. My husband said that it is not the right time for me to reestablish myself in the workplace."

Unlike Pamela, many mothers are ready to return to employment, sometimes with careers that differ from their previous ones. "When the children were young, I had a lot in common with the other moms, but now that the kids are in school full time, I feel that we are not as connected anymore. So now I am striving to obtain my teacher's certification," declares Jo Ann. "I plan to teach, using my free time in a more industrious way than getting my nails done. All my efforts are currently going to my class time and assignments."

Returning to the workplace on her own terms was Cynthia's goal. She started her own part-time marketing consulting company, running her firm from 8 a.m. to 1 p.m., Monday through Friday, in order to maintain contact with her young children. "At first, I was nervous that setting up my consulting company would be seen as a lark and not taken seriously by major corporations, my prospective clients. Yet once I received that first job, others seemed to follow one after another as I needed them. Being patient while starting up my company paid off, as it took six months of effort to land that first consulting engagement. There were times that I was offered more opportunities than I could handle and was forced to turn down clients that I knew would never call again, but I preferred that to running myself into the ground. Being able to call my own hours and stick to them was the basis for forming my own company—it certainly wasn't for the stability. Emotionally, I kept thinking that my luck would run out any day and that no more clients would call, but that never happened."

Cynthia wasn't the only mother who developed her own firm in order to obtain the paid hours that she desired. In June 2005, the *Wall Street Journal* stated that many middle-aged women started their own businesses as a way to formulate their own solutions. In fact, 10.6 million women-owned businesses exist in the United States, accounting for 19.1 million employed people.[4]

"PUSH, PULL" BETWEEN LIFESTYLES

Julie's story exemplifies the "push, pull" mothers have with employment. She yearned for a connection with her children yet at the same time loved her career with the status and income that it brought. Her story is one of moving from the workforce into the home and back into employment.

"Deciding to stay home was arduous—I loved both my career and family. But I was traveling five days a week and was so tired when I finally reached home that I did not interact with my children. I was so grumpy— why would they want to talk to me anyway? My husband had been a stay-at-home dad and was recently offered a big opportunity, which made my being at home financially possible. While I could not afford to resign forever, nor did I want to, I could swing stopping work for a few years. I knew that bonding with my two children when they were young was important, so I decided to take a chance and ask my company for a leave of absence, giving me the ability to stay home and experience what it was like to be an at-home mother. My company was wonderful, granting me a two-year leave of absence. Upon leaving, I knew that when I returned, I may not have the same position, but I will be at the same grade level.

"My initial days at home were full of surprises as I did not know what I was missing," claims Julie. "I had never seen backpack notes. I didn't know that I was supposed to sign up for the PTA, I had been so disconnected from the schools. After just five months, I was already more in sync with my kids. As an at-home mom, my day is full, not luxurious, not eating bonbons. Work was mentally exhausting, but home is physically exhausting. My corporate work was a breeze versus this, but when at home I have no night sweats or overlying stress. I used to feel guilty about taking care of myself, but now I exercise regularly and feel great. Now I even have hobbies. Yet I must admit, I don't tell new people that I meet I'm a stay-at-home mom—I let them know that I'm on a two-year leave of absence. I miss being the only woman in first class, miss financial independence. I don't miss always being tired, that awkward feeling 'where do I fit in.' I love my house being put together and being connected with my kids. My company has always treated me well and is doing me a great favor to allow this leave of absence."

Julie adds, "Now that I have been home a full year, I am pining for the hustle and bustle of my office and the extra money that I could be earning. My job was my identity—no one did it for me. It was gratifying. When I am at home, the family has to pinch every penny, having no funds for those fun little extra expenditures. My motivation to unload the dishwasher or make dinner is low. It's as though I'm the maintenance department for the family, receiving no thank-yous, no raises, just questions regarding where the clean wash is. In fact, I have approached my company regarding returning earlier than planned, maybe in the next three months or so, as I have met my goals of a better understanding my two children. My husband will rein in his work so that he can be there for my children after school. The hardest part is sending my son back to a daycare center until 4 p.m. or so when my daughter arrives home from school. As I reenter the workforce, I will strive to maintain the rapport that I have been fortunate enough to develop with my two children over this leave of absence."

Cristine's story exemplifies teamwork with her husband, much the same as Julie, moving from part-time to full-time work for financial reasons and for the insurance family benefits. "My first child, Anne, was in daycare until her second birthday, when I had my second child, Judy. Since my law firm was in the start-up phase and I was not earning much, I began practicing law part time from home. Both girls were in the same part-time daycare center but in separate areas because of their ages. My husband resigned from his job about the time Anne was three years old and Judy was one year old. Up to this point, he had not spent any time with the girls because he had worked long days at his corporation and then restored an old home of ours at night. He left early, around 7 a.m., and returned late after they had gone to bed, around 10 p.m., never seeing the girls. His resignation related directly to wanting to be part of the girls' lives. Now he would become the childcare provider.

"Of the two of us, I had more earning potential upon expanding my business. Since I was making enough money to open my own office, I did so, increasing my hours. Unlike with my husband's prior career, I could arrange my own hours to take advantage of good weather in the spring, summer, and fall. On beautiful days, I could take a hike or go swimming or play in the park with my family, then return to finish up any remaining work later at night. So in 2002, I was running my own legal practice, earning the income for the family, and still coming home by 4:30 p.m. so I could take Anne and Judy to the park or to a local pool in the late afternoon.

"Then, I was offered a job with a corporation that was regular hours, 9 a.m. to 5:30 p.m. While the freedom of determining my own hours would be lost, it offered full coverage insurance, which I needed as I had been struggling with health insurance," Cristine continues. "On my own, I was using COBRA insurance, which was expensive. The insurance was a huge issue for me because Judy will need hip surgery in the future. In addition, the job provided a regular salary, which was better than the income I had been receiving in a fledging law practice. While my own practice was more interesting legal work and afforded more flexibility with the girls, I had to do what was right for my family and leave my own firm for the insurance and stability in compensation. The current job is less stressful, as I have no deadlines, but I miss the afternoon walks in the park with the girls."

I can't discuss reentries into the workforce without mentioning Brenda Barnes. Her resignation as president of the PepsiCola North American division in 1998, caused by her wishes to spend more time with her children, surprised and disappointed feminists, symbolizing for many that women can't have it all. But after working part time on and off over six years in order to get to know her three children better, she returned to the workforce full time in the summer of 2004 as president and chief operating officer of the Sara Lee Corporation, proving that it is possible for women to stop, take time out for their families, and reenter the workforce on their own timetables.

CONSIDERING A SWITCH

No matter what women choose as a lifestyle, the decision is never made lightly. Each mother interviewed had thought long and hard about life with various forms of employment before settling on her own current choice. And as with Julie and Cristine, life choices alter over time.

"Switching from full-time employment to staying home is a tough decision for anyone. As an at-home mother, you are appreciated much less than at the office by society. And every day, you start at square one with cleaning, cooking, and laundry, forcing you to structure your life with self-directed plans. I have a friend who has a 'grocery day' and a 'paying bills' day in order to remain sane. When I hear about all of this, it makes me nervous to quit, so I continue with my office schedule while wondering what an at-home life would be like," says Laura.

Chris builds on Laura's thoughts. "I was sold on working when I came out of college, never considering staying at home, even after childbirth. My perspective did not change through my daughters' elementary or middle school years. But now, as my children are entering high school, I'm not getting a charge out of my career the way I used to. The classic response to outside motivation is not exciting me anymore . . . the status of earning the income . . . the title of my job . . . the satisfaction is not what it was when I was younger. I realize that my children are off to college in a few short years and time with them is running out, so I'm rethinking my options. My mortality is beginning to show."

NOTES

1. Based on interviews.

2. Patricia Cohen, "Mothering and Its Cultural Discontents," *New York Times* (March 24, 2004): E7.

3. Based on interviews.

4. Carol Hymowitz, "Women Often Discover Their Business Talent after Kids Are Raised," *Wall Street Journal* (June 14, 2005): B1.

NINE

WHY NOT CO-PARENT?

Most marriages have not changed much in the last forty to fifty years—the majority of men don't wash the clothes, attend to the children, prepare meals, vacuum the house, or dust furniture. Mom still does it all while, many times, also bringing home income. It is almost an assumption that women will compromise their vocations for their husbands' careers.

Debbie believes, "To advance in the world requires women to become men, with few exceptions in certain career areas. Women can succeed in the lower ranks, but it's difficult at the top with a family. This male orientation to the workplace has caused women to pull out. They ask themselves, 'Do I really want to be a man or retain my identity as a woman and a mother?' *Men* are not expected to scale back their hours or quit when they start a family, just *women*. Mom is the one handling daycare issues, finding childcare, and regulating its quality, not Dad."

Why is it that Mom steps aside and not Dad? Why does Mom maintain two jobs, while Dad has one?

Employed mothers resent at-home mothers who hold down one job, having all day to attend to family chores and duties, while they only have a few hours an evening. And mothers at home hold rancorous feelings toward working-out-of-the-house mothers because they gave up their career identities, becoming, at times, little more than glorified housekeepers to keep their families running smoothly. Marriages have changed little for women regarding household chores and raising the children, while employment status for women is very different than it was forty years ago. A major step in breaking down the Wall is altering how housework and caring for children is split between the father and mother, giving mothers the opportunity for time with their children as well as their careers. Splitting the household duties between spouses will help eliminate that "push, pull" feeling mothers have for employment and eradicate guilt regarding the children.

THE WALL BETWEEN WOMEN

MARRIAGES NEED MODIFICATION

"All the women that I know are still responsible for the home and the house-work, whether they are employed outside the home or not," says Martha, whose views reflect those of a majority of the women I interviewed. "Men have full-time occupations yet are not the ones to pick up the family room or prepare the dinner or change the beds. The ultimate responsibility always falls on the woman. Home is recuperative for the children and the father, but not the mother—it's work for her. The father and children go home after their daily activities and unwind, yet Mom never relaxes at home. At nine at night, she may still be found driving children home from karate class or throwing in one more load of laundry. She rests only when she is so sick that she cannot carry the pasta pot to the stove."

Why do women let this happen to them? Why is it that "a husband works from sun to sun, but a woman's work is never done?" Martha says that when she was fifteen years old, she baby-sat for a family whose mother was the major breadwinner. The mother gave Martha the food list, the laundry list, the children's chores, and activities for the day—everything. Even as a teenager, Martha always wondered why the dad, who had more time, didn't do it.

Shirley Sloan Fader, author of *Wait a Minute, You Can Have It All*, refers to this as one of the "one-paycheck family" rules. A mother's success as a woman depends on her doing the parental work and doing it properly. If the children and home appear to have inadequate attention, she will be criticized as a bad wife and mother. Sloan Fader points out that this rule loads guilt onto the employed mother, who can't possibly meet this old one-paycheck standard.[1]

Another story comes from Danielle, who empathizes with her sister. "My sister, Karen, gets up at 3:30 a.m. to be at work at 5 a.m. She works six hours, arriving home at 11 a.m. so that her daughter has only four hours of daycare. Her career is compromised because she keeps part-time hours, making her unpromotable. At the end of the day, Karen goes to bed between 9 and 10 p.m., getting up at 3:30 a.m. again the next day. She has been on this schedule for years and is exhausted. I respect Karen for her priorities and am sympa-thetic because she is falling apart. She hasn't had a decent night's sleep for eleven years. On top of her draining schedule, she also does all the 'invisible work' that women always do—laundry, dishes, everything. Karen's life has been shortened by her home chores, schedule, and sheer exhaustion. Yet her husband, who is doing a minuscule amount of work in comparison, feels put upon by getting the kids ready in the morning and putting them on the bus. Men perform only one job. It's not fair.

"We have not made it easy for employed mothers, as quality daycare is hard to find and expensive," Danielle continues. "This affects women's, not men's, jobs, as they are always compromising for the betterment of the children. Systematically, few United States corporations have made the combination of employment and motherhood a livable existence for women. There are few, if any, systems to aid mothers, causing their home lives to bleed into the workplace. Employed mothers must choose their own compromises; they must make trade-offs. Generally speaking, fathers are not in the same position and make no compromises."

Traditional roles of mothers caring for the home and children, with fathers earning the money to pay for food and shelter, are hard to break, even when mothers have their own occupations earning income.

Jennifer, a copywriter from Denver, claims that her husband can't function while watching the children. "When I leave my husband alone with the kids for a few hours, nothing happens. The children are safe and that's about it—nothing happens in the kitchen or with the laundry, absolutely nothing. Once, when I took my family with me to a conference in Arizona, I left him with both of the children, while I went shopping. He had a difficult time feeding them lunch and a tougher time getting them down for a nap. He could barely handle them. When I returned, I asked where the car keys were, and he had no idea. After searching for an hour, we finally found them in the car door in the parking lot. That's very unusual for him to misplace things, the kids distracted him that much. On the other hand, he expects me to run the house, keeping everyone clothed, fed, and clean, while simultaneously watching the children and holding down a job without becoming flustered or upset. It would be nice if he would help out occasionally."

Over a third of the mothers report unprompted, "I can't count on him to help with the children—I must care for them all alone." For some women, this is because of their spouse's high level of unpredictable professional traveling, while for others it is their spouse's lack of interest with the children's activities. Others declare that their spouses are helpful when they are around, but their husbands are home so infrequently because of their long office hours that they never expect any assistance.

Diane's view is the same as that of several moms. "My husband is a physician, and when he is home, he is a big help. But when he is not here, he is not here, which is most of the time."

Irisa claims that her husband is there so infrequently that she feels like a "single mom with benefit of second income and health insurance."

Wistfully, Jennifer, along with others, says, "Someday maybe husbands and wives can be co-breadwinners with an equal distribution of pain-in-the-ass stuff and careers and kids' needs as far as access to parents is concerned. Co-parenting is not 'in' yet with society—it's still just Mom."

CHANGE IS POSSIBLE

Change is a necessity as the employed workweek is longer for everyone, both Mom and Dad. For a dual-career couple with children under age eighteen, the combined workplace hours have grown from eighty-one hours per week in 1977 to ninety-one hours in 2002, according to the Families and Work Institute.[2] Ann Crittenden, in *The Price of Motherhood*, reports that the average workweek has crept up to almost forty-eight hours for professionals and managers, while the so-called part-timer is now putting in close to forty hours per week.[3]

These longer hours, even for part-timers, are forcing the need for a change in roles. And in a small minority of marriages today, change is occurring. Through the interview process, I talked to five mothers who are the primary breadwinners in their households whose husbands manage the family. Three of these mothers have stay-at-home husbands, and the other two are married to men who changed careers, becoming the primary parent, so that mom could focus on her career and become the principal wage earner. I talked to yet another woman who let her full-time employed husband handle their four children during the workweek, while she flew to her office located in a different city to fulfill her duties. And most striking, I discussed this topic with another mother who was part of a couple where *both* parents are engaged in part-time work in order to share caregiver duties.

At-Home Fathers

In the 1980s, Linda, a new mother at the time, discussed with me how her husband, Al, could be a terrific stay-at-home dad. Business-oriented tasks did not thrill Al. He received no rush from a presentation well done or a plan well executed. However, he loved to cook elaborate meals and to develop and upkeep intricate gardens and was generally a homebody, a perfect at-home father. Linda, on the other hand, was enraptured by her career, flourished under pressure, and savored business challenges. Being a family with a stay-at-home dad had appeal to both of them, yet it wasn't even a consideration at the time because of the social implications.

But today, a few dads *are* starting to stay home with their sons and daughters. According to the 2002 Census Bureau, of the 5.3 million parents with children under age twelve who stay home to care for their children, 105,000, or roughly 2 percent, are fathers.[4] This change of Dad staying home instead of Mom is evolving from the desire to have a balance of work and pleasure within the family while also trying to maximize income. The parent with either the most energy for employment or the highest income potential, regardless of gender, becomes the major breadwinner, enabling the other parent to become the primary caregiver. As fathers appreciate their stay-at-home wives who raise the children, mothers equally value the care that their husbands who stay home give their sons and daughters. These fathers are removing huge emotional burdens from their wives by attending to the family. Activities occupying only mothers in the past are now also being performed by at-home fathers. These include positions on the board of PTAs, attending playgroups, tutoring in classrooms, and even becoming Girl Scouts. Yes, I know a dad who ran the cookie sale for his daughter's Girl Scout troop in Connecticut.

"Having my husband, Adam, at home makes a big difference for me," claims Anne, a vice president of a promotion corporation. "Since my son, Zach, was in kindergarten, he has been an at-home father. Adam was forced to leave a job that he loved to relocate with me as I am the primary bread-winner in the family. My son needed continuity at home because he was moved several times prior and put in the new kid role often. I'm lucky because Adam involves himself in Zach's school, participates in his sports activities, and runs the household. *He* interacts with the at-home mothers, not me, because he is the at-home parent. If I could, I would switch places with Adam in a minute. I admit, I'm a little jealous of stay-at-home parents because I have a real appreciation for what Adam does."

Mothers as well as fathers have to adjust to the new roles they create when Dad stays home. They have no mentors to show them how to maneuver through the obstacles thrown in front of them. As with all trailblazers, these couples are greeted by snide comments and put-downs when others learn of their role reversals. Yet as Karen says, they muddle through the nasty remarks by maintaining a united front.

"My husband, Jim, is a stay-at-home dad," states Karen, a director of manufacturing at a Fortune 100 corporation. "People react weirdly to his status, not knowing what to say or how to handle it. Some say that they can't believe my situation, and men, in particular, put my husband down badly. Several men have said to me, 'He must be a bum. Why don't you dump him and come with me?' Other men have said that they would love to be in the same situation, almost propositioning me, 'You can take care of me instead of him.' My bosses thought that Jim was a slacker, really prejudiced against him; it wasn't good for his ego. But we had handled it between us—we decided that he would stay home with my son, and I would be the wage earner. Jim is a great dad, not just a great husband. He cooks, cleans, grocery shops, washes clothes, and is even on the board of the PTA at my son's school. I could not have reached my position if Jim had not stayed home with my son. I had the ability to travel and work late without worrying how my son was doing or who was taking care of him."

Anne also ran up against issues at school that arise only with at-home dads. "There are many assumptions out there that are not real. The kindergarten teacher has a photo of each child and the parent that brought them to school on the first day up on the wall. Zach was with Adam because that is who bought him to school. One day when I came in, she took a second photo so that I, 'the mom,' was up on the wall with all the other mothers. Now, she didn't take second photos with all the other dads. It's just assumed that Mom stays home and runs the household. All the talk is about 'mom this' and 'mom that,' but at my house, *Dad* is the one at home managing the family."

Not only do these trailblazers have to fend off comments from others, but they also have to learn how to deal with the new situation themselves. Mom may be more of a fastidious housekeeper than Dad, expecting the laundry to be folded and put away, not just washed, with family members coming into the laundry room to look for clean clothes themselves. Each parent manages the household in his or her own manner. In the past forty years or so, the household was run by Mom and, therefore, operated to her liking by her methods. Whatever system of directing the household functions were, they were by Mom's design. But if Dad stays home, they are by his schematics. It takes getting used to.

"The first two years after having children, we both worked. Hunter worked part-time and I worked full time." Kathy, a vice president of operations, says, "Then, he stopped altogether, making me the wage earner. It helps me tremendously that my husband is home raising the children, allowing me to concentrate on my job without the distraction of 'what are the kids doing after school today?' Hunter is great with the kids and does all the fun stuff. He really focuses on them, takes them to the park, swims with them at the pool. But dads are different, and the house does not operate the same way it would if I was home. Dinner is not a priority, nor is a clean house. I have to come home and pick up after a full day of the children's fun and games. Homework gets done, but backpack notes go unread if I do not dig them out. Women are nesters; men are not."

Part-Time Employed Dads

Fallout from the women's revolution is the upheaval in the father's role, putting the family first. Men are beginning to struggle with the same concerns that women have wrestled with for the past thirty or more years. How is it possible to be a good father while holding down a lucrative, interesting career? Should a father refuse a promotion involving significant travel in order to be home for the children's softball games? How can Dad coach soccer and run the East Coast's sales division—is there enough time for both? While most men are still defined and restricted by their careers, some feel that they can come home now.

A small minority of couples has initiated this shift toward a partnership in earning income and caring for the family. Between the two marriage partners, they determine who has the best potential for a lucrative income stream, who enjoys the home front more, who gets a kick out of employment the most, who can handle the children's issues better, then they decide who will be the major breadwinner and who will be primary caregiver and, hence, secondary wage earner. After that, whether spoken or not, tasks become either his or hers, dependent on who is where, when, and who accomplishes what best.

Two mothers living states apart told me almost identical stories regarding their decisions to become the primary income earners and their husbands the significant caregivers. Both had husbands who were miserable in their high-powered, profitable occupations of choice. Each man desired to switch to a lower-profile vocation that afforded him more hours with his family.

Bridget's husband, Stan, was a successful lawyer on his way to becoming partner in his firm. Bridget, also an attorney, was practicing law part time in a large corporation, with two young children watched by a sitter at home. Employment with her corporation had been full time up to the birth of her second child, whereupon she requested part-time employment. When Stan told Bridget that he loathed his occupation, she supported him in his desire to return to school for retraining. Bridget's corporation reinstated her full-time employment status per her request, as she needed her entire salary in light of Stan's career adjustment. He went from being a sixty-hour-per-week attorney to a high school teacher. When their daughters come home after school, Stan is there to attend to their needs, making Bridget comfortable that her children are in good hands. Since he has reduced his working hours, not eliminated them, Stan and Bridget split up the chores, with Stan handling more tasks than Bridget. She grocery shops; he cooks dinner and washes clothes. He carpools his daughters and their friends to the girls' afternoon activities; she oversees homework at night, while he is grading papers.

Bridget retells her neighbors' reactions. "When I moved from part-time work back to full-time employment, stay-at-home mothers asked me why I was doing that. They said, 'Aren't you going in the wrong direction? Why are you letting your husband do that to you?' My husband was going back to school to do something that he really wanted to do. It was better for the whole family. He is no longer a miserable lawyer but a cheerful, fulfilled high school teacher."

Chris, a full-time corporate finance manager, whose husband changed careers much the same as Stan did, declares, "My husband, Don, had no appreciation of the 'invisible' housework until he started helping out. Now the chores are completed by his methodology, not mine, as Don completes most of them. But when I go home, I'm not planning to put my feet up. Since I worked part time in the past, I understand what he's going through and pitch in upon arriving home. Don prepares dinner; I throw in a load of laundry. Don checks the kids' homework; I balance the checkbook. We both spend lots of time with the children in the evenings—baths, stories, and bed. We have a better balance by sharing the kids, the housework, and all the home issues."

One couple had a unique solution for the work/balance issue. Both the mother and father hold part-time jobs so that each of them can experience raising and enjoying the children. According to Cynthia, a consultant from Oregon, "My husband, Matt, has three part-time positions—he is a part-time high school teacher, coaches two school sports, and is a part-time architect working from home when he is not at school. He was a full-time architect prior to receiving his teaching certificate. Both Matt and I work part time and parent part time, adjusting our hours to each other's schedules. Our situation is unusual in that we can shift our hours and income based on money needed or time that we want for ourselves." Talk about a marriage of the future—this is an open-minded couple willing to do whatever is necessary to ensure a family atmosphere.

Fathers Who Help in Nontraditional Ways

While most fathers who want to become more involved with their families are still employed full time, many of them have modified their working hours to enable them to spend more time with their children. *They* are beginning to feel that they are missing out on the joys of raising children and want to be with the family more often. Several women described the positive effects that their husbands' efforts with the children have had on their families.

"Harry, a physician, switched jobs because his old office hours were inconsistent with having a family. He worked most weekends and was regularly called out three nights in a row," says Barbara, a commodity trader. "After arriving home and changing clothes, he was called. Sitting down to dinner, he was called. In the middle of reading bedtime stories, he was called. Now he works from 6 a.m. to 5 p.m., is 'on call' only two days per week once every three weeks, *and* has two weekends a month off—much better hours for forging relationships with your children. It was hard to be a family when he was never home at night. He changed the way he practices medicine specifically to accommodate his children."

While a majority of women do not have spouses who switch jobs to reduce their hours or work from home, some have husbands who help out in nontraditional ways. Randi's husband always drives the children to and from childcare each day, giving her a chance to clean the breakfast dishes before heading off to work and get a peaceful start on dinner in the evenings. Heather's husband washes, folds, and puts away all the laundry.

"When I moved to a new company in 1998 with a promotion, I was in between sitters, so my husband took leave of absence from his job to watch my son for six months until we found a childcare provider," declares Jamie.

THE WALL BETWEEN WOMEN

These steps may not appear large but are definitely headed in the right direction for aiding mothers to find a better balance between employment and home life, reducing that "push, pull" feeling.

And these measures are good for not only Mom and Dad but also the children. According to Jerrold Lee Shapiro, a counseling psychologist and professor at Santa Clara University, Mom provides comfort and security when she cuddles her infant to her breast. Dad, on the other hand, positions the baby over his shoulder, facing out looking at his surroundings, or facing Dad himself, offering the idea of freedom and interaction with the world. When Mom plays with a young child, she reinforces creativity and self-esteem by letting the toddler lead the playtime activity. Dads typically direct the activities with youngsters, creating a sense of teamwork. *Both* styles develop well-rounded children.[5]

Kyle Pruett, a Yale University child psychiatrist, has found through his research that a father's involvement benefits the children. Those advantages include completing higher grade levels, increasing competencies in math for girls, gaining higher literary rates for boys, obtaining better problem-solving abilities for both sexes, and acquiring a higher level of moral sensitivity.[6] Additional involvement by Dad goes a long way.

SOCIETAL CHANGES

But most women are not as fortunate as those mentioned above—they either are constantly torn between their jobs and family on a daily basis, or they are at-home mothers yearning for something of their own. Patty's comments reflect the lives of many at-home moms: "My husband asked me if I was where I thought I would be at this stage of life. Doesn't he realize that I have altered all of my goals and aspirations to be home with the family? Even though I am lucky that I have the opportunity to stay home raising the boys and have a husband who supports my decision, I can't wait for the kids to graduate high school so that I can pursue my personal aspirations."

Kathy's thoughts echo the sentiments of numerous employed moms. "When you are a full-time employed mother, someone is always angry with you. If you are at the office, your kids are wondering why you are not at home making dinner. If you are at home, co-workers are irritated that the boss is letting *you* go home, while others are still there. You can't win."

Setting themselves apart from the majority of families today, the couples discussed in this chapter are on the forefront of societal change. They are ignoring past roles, implementing nontraditional lifestyles that enable them to succeed as a family. Mom is not sacrificing her career for Dad's occupation; Mom and Dad are performing one and a half jobs, each alongside each other, rather than Mom having two; or both parents are holding part-time jobs while sharing childcare duties. In these families, both *mother and father* are enjoying their role as parents because they have eliminated, or at least reduced, guilt and that "push, pull" for employment.

NOTES

1. Shirley Sloan Fader, *Wait a Minute, You Can Have It All: How Working Wives Can Stop Feeling Overwhelmed and Start Enjoying Life* (New York: G. P. Putnam's Sons, 1993), p. 32.

2. Families and Work Institute, "Highlights of the 2002 National Study of the Changing Workforce," http://www.familiesandwork.org/about/index.html (accessed June 9, 2005).

3. Ann Crittenden, *The Price of Motherhood: Why the Most Important Job in the World Is Still the Least Valued* (New York: Henry Holt, 2001), p. 260.

4. Market Probe International, "Prosumer Pulse 2004: A Global Study—Anticipating Consumer Demand," Conducted for EuroRSCG Worldwide (February 2004): The Modern Day Father: U.S. and U.K., p. 5.

5. Barbara F. Meltz, "Dads Are No Longer the 'Assistant Parent,'" *Boston Globe* (June 16, 2005): H1.

6. Ibid.

TEN

CULTURAL CHANGE NECESSARY

The bottom line is that women today are trying to cultivate a harmonious family atmosphere where the mother's individual activities—whether those include employment, hobbies, or volunteer work—mesh well with the day-to-day scheduling of family activities, enabling her to run the home as smoothly as possible. And while some moms may not reach their objectives, this is their sincere intention. The Wall's foundation is built because of cultural conflicts that expect women to be full-fledged employed participants in society *and* selfless mothers as well, forcing many mothers to choose sides. The Wall is then built up as each mother defends her own position, refusing to gain an understanding of how the other side lives.

Neither group leads the perfect life, as each side has its own positives and negatives. An employed woman has self-earned income and an identity but little time available for her family and almost none for herself. Stay-at-home mothers have time for their children, husbands, and friends but lack an identity and many times maintain isolating, debilitating routines. Clearly, having it all is not possible. There are always sacrifices for opportunities; each gain carries a loss to some degree.

Over half the mothers in the United States currently work outside the home, highlighting the fact that the Wall must be addressed. It can be torn down by targeting three specific areas. The first two are success and guilt. Each and every mother must determine what "success" is for her, not for her neighbor or sister or friend, but for herself. After that, and only after that, will she have the ability to abandon "mother's guilt." At this point, having found an internal balance or peace within themselves, mothers can now address the third point, supporting one another and tearing down the Wall.

REDEFINE SUCCESS

The new definition of success is balance—it is key for a mother's state of happiness. For the full-time worker, success may be having time to read bedtime stories to her four-year-old daughter each night, while success for an at-home mom may be running a plastic-recycling program in town. The appropriate balance between time spent on self-fulfillment, whether or not that is employment, versus time spent on the family varies for each individual.

"Time is a scale for everyone, at-home mother, full-time employed mom, or part-timer," says Tammy, a former accountant and current real estate agent. "You are happy when you are balanced between the various facets of your life—your social, creative, parental, and intellectual sides. If you have reached an equilibrium, then you are happy. But if there is a big skew in any one direction, your scale gets tipped off balance, and frustration sets in. I must keep my scale balanced so as not to be irritated and discontent." Tammy's observations regarding herself seem to hold true for most of the mothers I interviewed.

For stay-at-home mothers, frustration arises from a lack of intellectual stimulation, isolation in the home, and insecurities with self, leading to a sense of self-failure. Although the family may be running smoothly, numerous at-home mothers believe that they have failed themselves by sacrificing their own dreams and talents for the benefit of the children. Tammy's remarks address this. "You can't wait for something magical to fall in your lap—if you are dissatisfied, you must determine what is missing and address it. If you have lost your workplace identity, then develop a new one relating to your current situation, whether it is volunteer related, such as working with the church mission committee or being a homeroom mom, or interest related, such as a jewelry designing or training for a marathon. Make yourself someone you are proud of in your stay-at-home role. Stop thinking and feeling that 'Susie is better than I am because she maintains a job.' Be secure with yourself and the decisions that you have made—I *chose* to be a mom; I *left* Arthur Andersen behind. When staying home began to feel confining, I volunteered in the schools for social interaction and intellectual release. When that no longer fit my life, I began my real estate career, which blended well with my family situation. My life is a continual evolution based on my children's age, my personal growth, and my family's financial position. Whenever I felt out of balance, I reevaluated my life and realigned it, adjusting areas where I was unfulfilled, discontent, or in need. What I consider 'success' unfolded over time, with these constant adjustments serving me well."

Charlene agrees with Tammy. "Many stay-at-home mothers are unfulfilled, necessitating something to spend their time on. They need to find something they are interested in and execute it well. You need to support yourself before anyone else will believe in you. If you are frustrated, it will show through your aggravations with small setbacks in life. Little things will get to you, causing dissatisfaction and irritation, radiating unhappiness toward your family. But when you complete a job well, whatever it is, you will project confidence, generating an aura of happiness around yourself."

And part-time employment can aid in eliminating this frustration for some stay-at-home mothers. Today, existing social norms say that women's part-time employment and jobs creatively designed to allow women to spend more time with their children are temporary strategies. But because 40 percent of the young people currently being trained in specific career areas, such as law and accounting, are women, fluid innovative jobs designed by mothers will probably prove more successful in the future than in the past.[1]

In early 2004, Sylvia Ann Hewlett, an economist at Columbia University, organized a task force of fourteen companies and four law firms to discuss the "hidden brain drain" of mothers in 2004. They discussed ways and methods for workers to easily reenter, slow down, or accelerate their career paths.[2] While this did not work in the 1980s, probably because it was politically correct lip service that was never internalized by most corporations, now the numbers may very well be on the sides of families, causing flexible pathways to open for mothers.

While at-home moms must redefine success for themselves as individuals to reach their balance, full-time employed mothers must redefine success for themselves as mothers. They must allow themselves the luxury of not "doing it all" in order not to burn themselves into the ground. Exhaustion will cause them to be snippy and short with their children, generating exactly the opposite effect they desire.

Parent educator Susie Isaacs Kohl, author of *The Best Things Parents Do*, recommends a few tricks in managing a busy weekday evening. Try to buy a hot, balanced lunch for the children at daycare or have the sitter feed the kids a balanced meal midday, if possible. This gives Mom the ability to prepare a quick, easy dinner, such as bacon and eggs, soup, or tacos, without guilt. It makes the dinner hour less stressful and reduces clean-up afterwards. Kohl also advocates using commuting time home to relax. Listen to the radio if driving or read a newspaper if riding a train—don't make business calls. This is a transitional period into mom-mode. Kohl suggests another trick— spend the first twenty minutes in the house playing with the kids. This makes them less needy later when you are preparing dinner or ironing clean clothes for the next day.[3]

Women can also borrow some of employed mother Faye's ideas from chapter 4 as well. She uses lunchtime to make phone calls, organize her week, and run errands. She volunteers for *one* job that is meaningful to her, selecting it thoughtfully. With older children, such as Faye's, mothers can split the chores among family members, having one child run a load of laundry and another wash the dinner dishes. Children can be assigned age-appropriate jobs such as making their own beds, setting the table, watering the plants, or even dusting and vacuuming. Don't forget to give Dad a few items. Running the house is *not* Mom's sole responsibility—every family member should share in its operation. The family is in this together, so everyone *including* Mom can relax once the household tasks are completed. And if husbands are unable to lighten the load because they are out of town or working, skip the dusting this week or let the dishes air dry in the rack. Everyone will be happier.

To gain a feeling of intimacy with your children, Allie, a full-time worker herself, recommends an end-of-the-day ritual for each family member. For younger children, it could be something as simple as a bedtime story or playing with them in the bathtub, taking ten or fifteen minutes. With older children, it might be discussing the best part of their day while kissing them good night.

Mothers can also gain useful information from businesses that have been born out of the desire to aid them. Working Mother Media provides strategies and solutions for millions of moms. It includes *Working Mother* magazine and the corresponding Web site, which is full of tips and suggestions to help moms in their daily lives.

Another example is Dream Dinners (http://www.dreamdinners.com), a business that encourages families to connect around the dinner table with home-cooked meals. This business goes beyond recommendations and actually helps Mom execute her daily tasks. When attending a three-hour session, a woman will prepare ingredients for and package twelve uncooked dinners ready for the freezer, giving her three meals a week for a month. During the upcoming weeks, she will defrost them as needed and cook them according to the simple directions. Since all the cutting, chopping, and measuring has been completed ahead of time, she spends virtually no time preparing or cleaning up these meals, making midweek dinners a pleasure instead of a chore.

To create a better balance, some full-time mothers are turning to flexible working hours. Brandeis University researchers in Waltham, Massachusetts, conducted a study with J. P. Morgan Chase & Co. to quantify the relationship between after-school activity parental stress and job mistakes or disruptions. Parents were asked questions regarding stress specifically related to after-school care and safety. Brandeis's Community, Families & Work program researchers focused on this because of the mismatch of corporate hours versus the hours children attend school. Findings reveal that parents concerned about after-school arrangements are more likely to make on-the-job mistakes, miss an average of five days more of work per year than low-stress parents, and turn down extra work hours. The researchers are encouraging the use of the findings to support flexible working hours for parents.[4] Again, with the "hidden brain drain" coming into focus for corporations, especially in law and accounting, flexible schedules may be significantly more acceptable in the future.

Each mother must redefine what success is to *her* by determining how she can strike a balance in her life and then strive to attain it. Success to a stay-at-home mother may be leading the town's fund-raiser for a cancer cure or playing on the local club's tennis team. For a full-time employed mother, success may be having her husband wash the laundry so she can oversee seven-year-old Sam's homework or coach the Little League softball team. Since Mom's emotional attitudes translate directly to her children, a mother's happiness is important not only to her but also to her entire family.

One-third of all the mothers interviewed claim that either their schedule or job/family balance is the best part of their lives today. As Mary Ann, a former physician, says, "I have found a balance with raising two babies who are safe and clean and am glad that I am not ashamed to say, 'I am a stay-at-home mother.' I have nothing to show in the outside world right now, and that's okay." Or, as Barbara says, "I'm extremely blessed with my work situation and family atmosphere. I have flexibility with my job, allowing me to keep my hand in a career that I love while also allowing me to be home at a reasonable hour to make dinner and eat with the family. This is the best part of my life." Self-defined balance equals success for today's mothers.

ABOLISH GUILT

By addressing success, we can begin to alleviate guilt, the second area of improvement. Mothers are constantly questioning themselves about their sons and daughters: "Am I doing the right thing for my children?" "If I stayed home, would the children make better grades in school?" "If I had taken the job closer to home with less money, would the children be happier than they are now?" "How can I be the best parent possible?" Employed mothers torture themselves with these types of questions regularly, piling on "mother's guilt" because their homes are not like June Cleaver's, with fresh-baked cookies ready when the children arrive home from school. These mothers are holding themselves up to a 1950s gold standard that doesn't exist.

A woman's ability to be a good mother for her children hinges on the efforts she makes with her children, not on her status as full-time employee. Employment is *not* the gauge of motherhood's success or failure. Irisa, a project engineer, explains, "I think your comfort with yourself as an employed mother depends on the behavior of your kids, how they interact with adults, how they interact with other kids. If your kids are all right, you're doing okay. There are lots of dual-income parents where the children are not focused, not behaving well, and acting up in class. I have a family full of teachers who can pick them out all the time, and I can see it myself. Those are the parents not paying attention to their children after working hours at home in the evenings. As a working parent, you must set aside time for your children. It takes focus and effort. Coming home, kicking off your shoes, and turning on the television, hoping that the children can muddle through for themselves, is much easier than sitting down and reviewing homework with them. I stopped watching television years ago—I probably watch two hours of television a year. Every minute that I'm not at work, I am balancing my household duties to maximize time for my daughters. By giving my children as much time as possible, I have alleviated the 'employed mother's guilt.'"

Judy, a director of diversity who has always been a full-time employed mother, reads about working versus stay-at-home mothers' effects on their children. By perusing books written by experts on the subject, she has reached conclusions that aid her in releasing her guilt. "Sons and daughters of *both* types of mothers can grow up to be either solid, moral citizens or lazy goof-offs. The determining factor does not rest on the mother's employment as there are no conclusions leading to that. I think that it depends on the parents being content themselves and then producing happy children."

Judith Warner, author of *Perfect Madness: Motherhood in the Age of Anxiety*, agrees. "Studies have never shown that total immersion in motherhood makes mothers happy or does children any good. On the contrary, studies *have* shown that mothers who are able to make a life for themselves tend to be happy and to make their children happy. The self-fulfillment they get from a well-rounded life actually makes them more emotionally available for their children—in part because they're less needy."[5] Mothers who make an effort and spend time with their children, showing them that they care, *should have no guilt.* If mothers are content and happy with themselves, they will pass that fulfillment on to their children, giving their sons and daughters a sense of satisfaction with their own lives. This knowledge should alleviate all possible "mother's guilt."

"Mother's guilt," usually associated with employed moms, is also felt by at-home mothers. For these women, guilt revolves around today's implications that you rob society of your talents if you do not use your education. Colleen, an at-home mother, says, "Lots of at-home mothers feel that they must be a martyr at home to justify not bringing in any money. If they are home, this guilt factor almost requires that they sacrifice themselves for everyone else because they are not earning any income."

Sharon agrees. "Most moms are well educated where I live and feel guilty if they have a good education and they are not using it, sort of short-changing themselves and society. Yet if you are a working mom, you believe that you are shortchanging your children. Everyone feels guilty either one way or another, even though we are *all* making sacrifices."

All mothers must release this "mother's guilt." We can liberate ourselves by realizing that the gold standard in mothering from the 1950s doesn't exist. We must abandon this pursuit of parenting perfection and fulfill our role as parents and members of society to the best of our abilities. This release benefits not only mothers but also their families.

A software executive for a Fortune 100 corporation, Shami claims, "Women whom I have chosen to be friends with are terrific and accomplished. I know one woman who is a Girl Scout leader and on the town library board. She was a Harvard graduate—never worked—yet she wants her daughters to meet women in business. These stay-at-home mothers are intelligent and accomplishing goals in life; they have formed an identity for themselves outside of the workforce and are self-confident."

THE WALL BETWEEN WOMEN

When a woman has underlying guilt about her choice, a mother on the "other side" brings out those feelings. That is why we dislike her—the dissimilar mother's very presence makes us feel bad about ourselves, even though she has said nothing. She makes us wonder about our own choices. Author of *Maternal Desire: On Children, Love, and the Inner Life*, clinical psychologist Dr. Daphne de Marneffe claims that women often build an inflexible identity for themselves as a way to deal with guilty feelings of not fulfilling the ideal roles of mother and worker: "In order to cope with the things we give up, we try to shore ourselves up."[6]

This guilt reinforces our forming a rigid self-identity, and we want to elevate ourselves over the "other mother," saying, "I am the better woman." According to Judith Stadtman Tucker of the Mothers Movement Online, an organization that helps mothers to connect to one another, "The smug sense of superiority that comes from denigrating another mother's values can be very seductive. Over and over and again, that's exactly where mothers get hung up."[7]

Enola Aird of the Motherhood Project, a national coalition to promote change for the betterment of children and families, believes that one way to break the Wall down is "to realize that most mothers today are on a continuum. Sometimes we are at work, sometimes we are at home, and then we're back at work again; it's not 'us' against 'them.'"[8]

By abolishing guilt, by not projecting our personal values onto others, and by realizing that the choices that are right for ourselves and our families are not always right for others, we will be able to stop judging dissimilar mothers. Eliminating guilt is a major step in breaking this vicious cycle of judgment and knocking out a big chunk of the Wall. When we are open to mothers who choose differently than we do, we are able to support one another, making friendships with those on "the other side," and life better for all of us and our children.

SUPPORTING THE "OTHER SIDE"

"My stay-at-home friends make me feel that I am doing a better job as a mother than I might think. They let me know that I am on the right track," explains Jillian, a respiratory therapist. "Since society wants us to be at-home mothers, employed moms want validation for doing the right thing. When I realize that I am on the same path with my sons as the at-home moms are with their children, I don't feel threatened by them. I may have if I was younger, but experience in life helps."

Edith, a university professor, agrees. "Dialogue is important, which causes me to change my views over time."

If women could accept each other for who they are, they could learn from one another and validate each other's choices. Supporting some mothers' requirements to maintain employment for financial or self-fulfillment reasons and other moms' needs to stay home for lifestyle or emotional reasons is necessary to break down the Wall. And the Wall *can* be broken down, as I heard success stories from a few mothers, particularly those on the West Coast, and I've even seen it on a television show.

The *Dr. Phil* television show ran a two-part series, "Mom versus Mom," giving us a dynamic example of breaking down the Wall. The first and second parts were taped at the same time, with the audience members seated according to their employment status. The first part focused on aiding two mothers in deciding whether or not they should work outside the home. Part 2, however, centered on the animosity between employed versus at-home mothers. While the show was clearly set up to highlight the discord between the two groups, and "mom bashing" did occur, the conclusion was harmonious, with Dr. Phil saying, "It's clear that both sides of this issue want the same thing. They want children that are healthy and happy and nurtured."[9]

Remember Irisa from the West Coast? Remember her comments regarding the fact that most mothers are employed either part time or full time in California because of the exorbitant cost of living and that mothers support one another? Or the part-time daycare options available to Lola in Oregon, which are rare in other areas of the country?

South Carolinian Carly says, "Among my neighbors, I was the only working mom when my children were young, but since I was running daycare from my home, the stay-at-home mothers could visit me during the week at my workplace. For example, if they went out to lunch, knowing that I couldn't join them because of my daycare responsibilities, they brought a meal back to me and sat with me, while the babies I cared for were sleeping. At-home mothers respected me and valued my work. I treasured those friendships."

Women must recognize that each mother follows the correct path for herself, even if it varies from their own. Cynthia, a part-time consultant, believes part of the barrier has to do with when women had children. She had her child when she was in her thirties. Cynthia had already had a career and was ready to stay home with her child, pursuing her occupation on a part-time basis. Even though her friends could not understand why Cynthia resigned her full-time job so easily, it was right for her.

Women having children in their twenties while moving up the corporate ladder may have an easier time balancing work and children than new mothers already in upper management who had children later in life and are expected to stay late whenever necessary or travel on short notice. Conversely, some women may have assistance in their households, enabling them to carry a heavy workload at the office and still have time for their children in the evenings. Women should endorse each other's decisions as Donna and Terri do.

Donna, a recruiter by day and a karate studio owner by night, supports all mothers. "I don't know of any mothers who are not working. If they don't work for money, they are performing tasks elsewhere such as within the PTA. I approach all mothers as if they are working full time. Taking a salary and being part of the workforce are not the same—just because you do not get paid for what you do, does not mean that you are not working."

Terri, a part-time faux painter, says, "I set up everything when I socialize with full-time career moms and their spouses, otherwise they would not socialize at all. I host three-quarters of the dinner parties at my house, or we go out to restaurants. They are very grateful to me for including them in my plans."

"My sister-in-law needs to return to work for financial reasons after being an at-home mom for a few years. She doesn't know anyone that is a full-time working mother that she respects as a mom," claims Joy, a chemical engineer. "I, however, have her respect as a part-time employed mother and have been slowly ramping up my hours over the last few years. I am up to working twenty-five hours per week now, so I am trying to coach her through the fact that being a working mom is okay. She really values my opinion and has been talking to me about it."

Some groundbreaking organizations are not only supporting all mothers but actually trying to bring them together as Joy does on her own with her sister-in-law. These groups are completing the business feminism left undone, getting mothers into the offices, but not addressing their motherhood needs or issues. Today's moms, who either reluctantly choose to leave the office to raise their families or struggle to balance work and family simultaneously, want to see women succeed in both arenas. They are part of such organizations as:

- Mothers and More (http://www.mothersandmore.org), a nonprofit organization that cares for the caregiver, helping mothers connect to one another, while they move through transitions that affect family, work, and life.
- The National Association of Mothers' Centers (http://www.mothers center.org), an organization that addresses needs of both employed and stay-at-home mothers by offering a network of programs to nurture the nurturers with emotional and physical support.

Even the National Parent Teacher Association (PTA) is among those groups, and it encourages volunteerism from *all* mothers by designing flexible volunteer opportunities that can be accomplished in as little as a half hour and by timing some events around the traditional workweek hours instead of the school day. Those successful events are exemplified by family fun nights comprising arts and crafts, movies, or games held at schools when full-time employed parents can attend. Another method of encouraging all moms to participate in the PTAs is by moving some meetings to gatherings already in progress. This was done by an Oregon PTA at soccer fields, taking advantage of the time when children were warming up for their games.[10] Obviously, the Wall won't be knocked over all at once but dismantled brick by brick, as exemplified by individuals such as Joy and organizations such as the Mothers and More.

PROFESSIONAL SUPPORT

As discussed earlier in chapter 4, many full-time employed mothers do not get support from each other even in the workplace. Numerous moms feel discriminated against after having children. So part of breaking down the Wall includes professional mothers banding together to improve the working environment for each other. Professional mothers who compete in the same organization for promotions can support one another—or tear each other down. If they perceive a fixed number of "female slots" available, the competition at the office is intense, leading to destructive rather than supportive behavior.[11]

This competition can cause mothers to feel trepidation when they leave early for their children's soccer games or to be intimidated into not asking for flexible hours or never going home on time because a "good worker stays late." This rivalry obviously impacts family life since it goes beyond the quality of work and spills into overtime—Mom's time to interact with her family. Experienced mothers can become mentors to younger women, while new moms can encourage seasoned mothers to become role models. Working together from many levels within an organization, mothers can requisition flexible scheduling, request part-time options, and rehire at-home mothers returning to the workplace.

Amy, a vice president of finance in a large corporation, tells how she and a female co-worker overcame this struggle, an excellent example of women successfully changing the norm. "Female relationships are dynamic—they can be destructive or a big benefit. Ruth was from a bank, I was from an investment firm, and we had both recently moved into corporate finance, wanting to get ahead. Feeling that the company was going to promote just one of us, we went after each other head on, aiming to ruin the other's career. To my surprise, Ruth came to me one day and said, 'We can either destroy each other or join forces to rise in the corporation together.' Battling one another hadn't been advantageous, so we decided to help each other out. Initially, we had honest discussions regarding compensation, what worked versus what did not work for us in the corporate environment, and what positions we were striving to attain. We realized that we were working harder and harder to get promoted and decided that instead we should be operating smarter. So we decided to network like the 'big boys.' Since we were both directors at the time, we established a group comprising many female presidents and vice presidents from our industry whose goal was networking and sharing.

"In the group, we discussed resumes, our own personnel files, executive coaching, recruiters, gender lawyers [lawyers who represent people, usually women, who have not been promoted, fired, or hired because of gender bias or people who make sexual harassment claims], bonuses, and salaries. Who was missing what in her background to get promoted, how to get to the next level—that was the essence of many of our gatherings. All of us brought in our personnel evaluations to review with one another, and we all had one thing in common—we were considered too aggressive and bitchy. Men never see that on their evaluations. Together we know what positions are open in which corporations, what opportunities are the best. We point each other in the right direction. And because of this organization, I know other women on business calls where I have never done business. The men stand there, scratching their heads, wondering, 'How do they know each other?' Support goes beyond the office as well—we assist each other with childcare, as we have a 911 number to call for emergency nannies when someone's sitter quits unexpectedly. I believe that we share at a level much higher than men.

"The structure of the group was based on a Christy Whitman management team model. So far, we have been together over ten years, maintaining a membership of about fifteen, really helping each other out by using honest communications. This is a great model of successful female relationships. It all comes down to how the individual feels about herself.

"I must admit, some women have bitten us. One woman took information back to management in my company, resulting in one of the group members being fired. So now we are very careful whom we include because honesty and trust are foremost. We are comrades collaborating with the dependable, reliable co-workers. Once the barrier between us is broken down, the satisfaction is great."

Just like Amy and Ruth, other women have also started organizations giving workplace tips and support. They include:

- 9 to 5 (http://www.9to5.org), the National Association of Working Women, strives to strengthen women's economic positions by focusing on family-friendly policies and eliminating workplace discrimination.
- Catalyst (http://www.catalystwomen.org) is a leading organization in researching and advising flexible scheduling for women.
- The Families and Work Institute (http://www.familiesandwork.org) is a nonprofit center for research that provides data on the changing workforce, family, and community. In 2004, it worked to increase employees' access to workplace flexibility.
- Blue Suit Mom (http://www.bluesuitmom.com) is devoted to creating balance between career mothers and their families.
- Worknmom (http://www.worknmom.com) was developed to help women balance a career and a life without guilt.

AN EXAMPLE FROM THE MILITARY

An excellent example of supporting each other, whether professionally or on a personal level, comes from within the US military. Since the military has historically moved families every two years, it has developed built-in, ongoing programs for emotional and moral support. Military wives whom I interviewed spoke of these assistance programs favorably. While these activities are tailored specifically to military needs, women can adopt the aspects of the programs that are appropriate in neighborhood settings, such as utilizing an information tree to pass along good news in the neighborhood. It is an ideal way to support one another regardless of whether one is employed.

"When your spouse is in the military, you are moving every two or three years to new locations where you have no family and know no one," claims Paula. "Military wives actually have formalized a network to support one another called the Key Volunteers. Years ago it was called Key Wives, but now is referred to as Key Volunteers because a spouse in the military can be either a husband or a wife.

"In a good military base, there is an excellent support system on or off base. There are two support trees, a social call tree and an information tree. The information trees starts with a commanding officer calling the Family Readiness Officer [FRO], who then calls the co-coordinator, who starts the phone tree. This is used for pertinent information such as when CNN has a breaking military news story, and none of the spouses on the base knows who was in that particular news location. It's a way to pass information about the husbands and wives in military action back to the base quickly, calming everyone down. The information tree passes along good information too, such as when someone is having a baby. Information is passed via the phone as well as via e-mail, depending on the urgency of the message.

"The social tree is separate, used for planning dinners, throwing birthday parties, or going to the movies for those whose spouses are not home, as you can't sit home watching television every night for nine months or more. It can also be utilized when spouses are home as well. The military has good social outlets—ice cream socials, family day BBQs—it's much nicer in the military than out of the military because you have a built-in social system wherever you go. Socializing is big in order to keep the nonmilitary spouse happy. Because if the spouse is happy, then the military personnel is happy.

"The Key Volunteers go beyond just passing along information and planning social events. They help in emergencies, much the same as a family would. Since the enlisted personnel are not paid well, there is a good chance that if someone's car breaks down, the spouse at home may not have enough funds to cover the expenses necessary to fix the car. This military spouse can call the Key Volunteers, knowing that they will help get her the resources that she needs.

"From your social group in the military, you may develop close friendships that replace your extended family," Paula adds. "Since you are nowhere near your family and have no grandparents or siblings to help with the children, mothers really need this. Moving often also makes it hard to acquire long-term baby-sitters—either you are transferring, or your babysitter is relocating to another base. The military is trying to slow down the transfers to save money, from two years to four years, but even if I stay, my friends can move. The Key Volunteers has given me more support and a better social life than what I would have outside the military."

CHANGING OUR CULTURE

While speaking to the many women who contributed to this book, I heard mothers who are confused over what to tell their daughters regarding work and motherhood. Danielle says that, based on her own experience as a software expert and mother, "Your college diploma should say, 'Warning: You can't do it all.' Reflecting on everything, I am most perplexed about what advice I should give my daughter. I don't know what to say, I don't know what to wish. . . ."

Lindsey, a part-time senior product manager, agrees. "When I was in college, I thought that I could have it all. I had these expectations that are impossible to fulfill. If you want the big career, you sacrifice the family. I have female friends who are high-ranking executives that all have family issues. It is rare to have a high-ranking woman who is either not divorced or without children in my industry. But when you support the family, your career is compromised and suffers. Life is full and rich on both sides—it is like comparing apples to oranges, yet I can't have both. Unlike men, I have to choose."

"Our society says that you can have it all and do it all without compromising, but that's not true," says Heather. "The quality of family life is compromised if both parents are running full steam ahead with their careers. But if the quality of family life is a high priority, then one parent's profession, usually Mom's, is compromised. Our culture must change."

But how do we change it? While many authors and groups advocate changing laws to improve families' lives, structural changes in our culture usually come from the ground up rather than from the top down. Laws are written to change what has already become the social norm. Each of us has the power within ourselves to change society by individually altering our own lives in the manner best for ourselves and our families. Laws will not bring about change—we as individuals will. Just as Anne, Adam, Karen, and Jim have turned the tables by having Dad stay home rather than Mom. Or as Martha is by running her own recruiting and consulting business three days per week, changing our view of the successful business woman. Or as Elaine is by completing her clinical drug research job in thirty-two hours per week versus the traditional forty and, therefore, revising the definition of a workweek.

Warner says in *Perfect Madness*, "Imagine how productive it would be if we stopped obsessing on the morality of staying home versus working and focus instead on the material conditions that stress all mothers to the point where they flounder and drown in The Mess. First of all, we would find that working mothers and stay-at-home moms' interests, ambitions, goals, and needs were strongly aligned."[12]

Judith Stadman Tucker declares, "The bottom line is that American mothers—whether or not they combine paid work and family, regardless of marital status, race or class—are all stuck in the same leaky boat. We can make matters worse by trying to shoot each other in the foot, or we can learn to respect our differences and concentrate on building a better boat."[13]

By redefining success and abolishing guilt, mothers can drop the emotional baggage that has prevented them from supporting one another. We can direct cultural change *ourselves*, breaking down the Wall by moving beyond personal assaults and banding together to gain more power over our employment, our family relationships, and ourselves. Since women are half the population, we *can* do it. We *can* put our biases aside and see each other for who we really are, sharing the realities of today's motherhood, not the idealized version of motherhood from the 1950s or the feminist "I can bring home the bacon and fry it up in the pan" version from the 1970s.

This is the answer to Danielle's question as to what to tell her daughter, Eve. Convey to her that there is no one "right way" to be a mother, but many options for successful motherhood. Show Eve the varied pathways that others are taking so that she can determine the best road for herself and her family. And then, most importantly, communicate to Eve the importance of keeping her defenses down and her mind open so that she can transform our culture, reaping the benefits from a true sisterhood.

NOTES

1. Louis Uchitelle, "Job Track or 'Mommy Track'? Some Do Both, in Phases," *New York Times* (July 5, 2002): C1.

2. Claudia Wallis, "The Case for Staying Home: Caught between the Pressures of the Workplace and the Demands of Being a Mom, More Women Are Sticking with the Kids," *Time* (March 22, 2004): 56.

3. Eilene Zimmerman, "Change Your Life Tactics for Achieving More Balance: Switching into Mom-Mode," *Sales and Marketing Management* (July 2004): 66.

4. Anne Marie Chaker, "Stressed Parents Report On-the-Job Problems," *Wall Street Journal* (March 23, 2004): D2.

5. Judith Warner, *Perfect Madness: Motherhood in the Age of Anxiety* (New York: Riverhead Books, 2005), p. 133.

6. Kim Pletichen, "The Mommy Wars: The Case for a Ceasefire," http://www.mothersmovement.org/features/cease_fire/cease_fire_pl.htm (accessed January 21, 2005).

7. Ibid.

8. Ibid.

9. *Dr. Phil*, "Mom versus Mom: Part II," episode 346, first broadcast September 3, 2004.

10. Sue Shellenbarger, "The Night Shift: Schools, PTAs Create Ways to Involve Working Parents," *Wall Street Journal* (December 2, 2004): D1.

11. Phyllis Chesler, *Woman's Inhumanity to Woman* (New York: Thunder's Mouth Press/Nation Books, 2001), p. 336.

12. Warner, *Perfect Madness*, p. 153.

13. Pletichen, "Mommy Wars."

1. Have you personally felt the Wall?

   • When?
   • How old were your children?
   • How did you react?

2. Did you see some of yourself in the book? Where?

3. Did the book open your eyes to the world of the mother on "the other side?" Why or why not?

4. Were you surprised by some of the quotations in this book?

   • Which ones?
   • Why?

5. Where in the continuum of working outside the home do you see yourself today?

   • Do you envision changing that in the future?
   • Does the age of your children affect your decision?

6. Did some sections of the book make you uncomfortable?

   • Which ones and why?
   • Did you resolve your comfort level by the end of the book? Why or why not?

7. What are your thoughts on the concept of mothers' lives constantly evolving based on the age of their children?

8. Do you envision becoming a better mother because you read this book? Why or why not?

DISCUSSION GUIDE

9. Since reading this book, are you more or less comfortable with your current status as a mother?

   • If you are less comfortable, do you plan to make changes to increase your satisfaction as a mother? If so, what are they?
   • If you are more comfortable, why?

10. Have you felt the Wall since reading the book?

    • Was your reaction different than it would have been before reading the book?
    • If so, what did you do differently?

Writing *The Wall between Women* was sheer enjoyment for me not only because I enjoyed the exploration of the topic, but more importantly because of the interesting and engaging conversations that I was privileged to hold with mothers across the country. If it were not for these women telling me their thoughts, feelings, and stories, there would be no book, no story to tell. My sincerest thanks and deepest appreciation go out to all of the one hundred and one mothers interviewed formally and to the other mothers who told me their stories informally as well.

My thanks go to my longtime, good friend from New Jersey, Sharon Russo, for being enthusiastic about the project from the very start. Without her backing, I wouldn't have had the courage to complete the first interview.

I also wish to thank my two sisters, Kathy Engelmann and Margo Searson, along with Bonni Brodnick. Kathy helped me in recruiting interviewees on the West Coast. Without those interviews, the geographic dispersion of the book would have been incomplete. Margo and Bonni reviewed and commented on my book proposal and query letters, providing invaluable comments that inspired publishers to request my manuscript.

Thanks to the initial readers of the book, Alison Prenetta, Cynthia Mayer, and Margo. Their support and reaction to the manuscript gave me the courage to mail the book to publishers.

Additional thanks go to Bob Zidle, for working with me to make the copying of the manuscript easy and time-efficient, as well as to Steve Neumann and Glenn Van Deusen, for helping me with my publicity campaign. I also want to thank Anne Hollows for supporting my project throughout the publishing process.

My gratitude goes to everyone at Prometheus Books for helping me through the steps of publication with ease. I couldn't have asked for a nicer group of people to publish my book.

ACKNOWLEDGMENTS

As for my teenage daughters, I appreciate their support throughout this entire effort. Ashley, thanks for your genuine enthusiasm upon learning that I had obtained a publisher, and Kelsey, thanks for the photography sessions, clicking away until you felt that you had a few winning shots for publicity photos.

And I especially thank my loving husband, Kurt, who stood behind me and endorsed my work throughout the entire process.

APPENDIX

RESEARCH DETAILS FOR THE WALL BETWEEN WOMEN

I developed a questionnaire to determine whether a Wall exists between employed and stay-at-home mothers. To make sure that I was obtaining what women really feel and not "politically correct" answers, I conducted each interview individually and promised interviewees anonymity.

Initially, I started interviewing a few women whom I knew personally in various parts of the country, and I asked them whether they could give me the names of two or three other mothers whom I could call. By using this process, I was referred to relatives and friends across the country. I randomly selected the referrals to call, ensuring that I had a large geographic dispersion. By using this methodology, I talked to women with a wide diversity of professions and backgrounds.

I called each woman and asked whether she would like to be interviewed for a book on women's issues. With those who answered yes, I set up a thirty-minute appointment at a time convenient for them. Despite the brief time frame for each appointment, the majority of interviewees talked for forty-five minutes to an hour.

Most interviews were conducted via the telephone. I started the interview by asking for demographic information—including the interviewee's name, address, highest level of education, household makeup, full-time work experience, part-time work experience, and so on. I assured each interviewee that her demographic information would be kept confidential and that I was using it for sorting purposes only. Then, I launched into the questionnaire, detailed below.

Because open-ended questions from more than a hundred interviews generated a lot of commentary, I entered all the responses into an Excel spreadsheet workbook. This enabled me to sort the raw data and draw conclusions from the many interviews.

QUESTIONNAIRE

"I am writing a book regarding women's issues, and I would like to ask you a few questions. I will be asking the same questions to over a hundred women across the United States. I would like for you to be totally honest and spontaneous with your answers. All of your answers will be anonymous, unless you would like to be quoted. I will ask that at the end of the interview. Ready?"

1. I believe that there is a "wall" between full-time working mothers and stay-at-home mothers. What is your reaction to that?
2. What do you think the image of the full-time working mother is?
3. What do you think the image of stay-at-home mothers is?
4. What do you think the image of the part-time working mother is?
5. Do you interact with full-time working mothers now? How?
6. How do full-time working mothers make you feel? Why?
7. Do you interact with stay-at-home mothers? How?
8. How do stay-at-home mothers make you feel? Why?
9. Do you interact with part-time working mothers? How?
10. How do part-time working mothers make you feel? Why?
11. *[For stay-at-home mothers only.]* If you worked full time when you had children, how were you treated by stay-at-home mothers then?
12. *[For stay-at-home mothers only.]* Why did you leave work?
13. *[For stay-at-home mothers only.]* When you were working full time, what was your daycare situation?
14. *[For part- and full-time working mothers only.]* Why do you work?
15. *[For part- and full-time working mothers only.]* What is your daycare situation?
16. What do you like best and least about your current situation?
17. Is there anything that you would like to add?
18. Would you like to remain anonymous?
19. Could you recommend the names of two or three others that I can call? Can I use your name as a way of introducing myself?

BOOKS

Aburdene, Linda, and John Naisbitt. *Megatrends for Women.* New York: Villard Books, 1992.

Beck, Martha N., PhD. *Breaking Point: Why Women Fall Apart and How They Can Re-Create Their Lives.* New York: Times Books, 1997.

Bravo, Ellen. *The Job/Family Challenge.* New York: Wiley, 1995.

Chesler, Phyllis. *Woman's Inhumanity to Woman.* New York: Thunder's Mouth Press/ Nation Books, 2001.

Chira, Susan. *A Mother's Place: Taking the Debate about Working Mothers beyond Guilt and Blame.* New York: HarperCollins, 1998.

Crittenden, Ann. *The Price of Motherhood: Why the Most Important Job in the World Is Still the Least Valued.* New York: Henry Holt, 2001.

De Marneffe, Daphne. *Maternal Desire: On Children, Love, and the Inner Life.* New York: Little, Brown, 2004.

Douglas, Susan J., and Meredith W. Michaels. *The Mommy Myth: The Idealization of Motherhood and How It Has Undermined Women.* New York: Free Press, 2004.

Fader, Shirley Sloan. *Wait a Minute, You Can Have It All: How Working Wives Can Stop Feeling Overwhelmed and Start Enjoying Life.* New York: G. P. Putnam's Sons, 1993.

Friedan, Betty. *The Feminine Mystique.* New York: W. W. Norton, 1963.

Hansen Shaevitz, Marjorie. *The Superwoman Syndrome.* New York: Warner Books, 1984.

Hays, Sharon. *The Cultural Contradictions of Motherhood.* New Haven, CT: Yale Press, 1996.

Kaminer, Wendy. *Women Volunteering: The Pleasure, Pain, and Politics of Unpaid Work from 1830 to the Present.* Garden City, NY: Anchor Press, 1984.

Kaufman, Loretta, and Mary Quigley. *And What Do You Do? When Women Choose to Stay Home.* Berkeley, CA: Wildcat Canyon Press, 2000.

Kitzinger, Sheila. *Ourselves as Mothers: The Universal Experience of Motherhood.* Reading, MA: Addison-Wesley, 1995.

185

BIBLIOGRAPHY

Kohl, Susan Isaacs. *The Best Things Parents Do: Ideas and Insights from Real-World Parents*. York Beach, ME: Conari Press, 2004.

Lewis, Susan. *Reinventing Ourselves after Motherhood: How Former Career Women Refocus Their Personal and Professional Lives after the Birth of a Child*. Chicago: Contemporary Books, 1999.

Matthews, Glenna. *"Just a Housewife": The Rise and Fall of Domesticity in America*. New York: Oxford University Press, 1987.

McCorduck, Pamela, and Nancy Ramsey. *The Futures of Women*. Reading, MA: Addison-Wesley, 1996.

McKenna, Elizabeth Perle. *When Work Doesn't Work Anymore: Women, Work, and Identity*. New York: Delacorte Press, 1997.

Ramming, Cindy. *All Mothers Work: A Guilt-Free Guide for the Stay-at-Home Mom*. New York: Avon Books, 1996.

Roberts, Cokie. *We Are Our Mothers' Daughters*. New York: William Morrow, 1998.

Swigart, Jane. *The Myth of the Bad Mother: The Emotional Realities of Mothering*. New York: Doubleday, 1991.

Tanenbaum, Leora. *Catfight: Women and Competition*. New York: Seven Stories Press, 2002.

Thurer, Shari L. *The Myths of Motherhood; How Culture Reinvents the Good Mother*. Boston: Houghton Mifflin, 1994.

Tracy, Laura. *The Secret between Us: Competition among Women*. Boston: Little, Brown, 1991.

Warner, Judith. *Perfect Madness: Motherhood in the Age of Anxiety*. New York: Riverhead Books, 2005.

Woolf, Henry Bosley, Editor in Chief. *Webster's New Collegiate Dictionary*. Springfield, MA: G. & C. Merriam, 1974.

MAGAZINES

Benne, Leslie. "Mom Envy: Think Other Parents Do It Better? How to Trust Yourself and Keep Jealousy at Bay." *Parenting* (November 1, 2003): 116.

Conlin, Michelle. "The Rise of the Mompreneurs: EBay Has Given Corporate Dropouts a New Way to Balance Work." *Business Week* (June 7, 2004): 70.

Jason, Sonya. "From Gunpowder Girl to Working Woman." *Newsweek* (February 23, 2004): 20.

Wallis, Claudia. "The Case for Staying Home: Caught between the Pressures of the Workplace and the Demands of Being a Mom, More Women Are Sticking with the Kids." *Time* (March 22, 2004): 50–57.

Williams, Joan C. "The Maternal Wall." *Harvard Business Review* (October 2004): 26.

Zimmerman, Eilene. "Change Your Life Tactics for Achieving More Balance: Switching into Mom-Mode." *Sales and Marketing Management* (July 2004): 66.

NEWSPAPER ARTICLES

Armour, Stephanie. "Some Moms Quit as Offices Scrap Family-Friendliness; Employers Cut back on Flextime, Job-Sharing." *USA Today* (May 4, 2004): 1.

———. "More Companies Downsize Family-Friendly Programs." *USA Today* (October 20, 2003): 1.

Chaker, Anne Marie. "Stressed Parents Report On-the-Job Problems." *Wall Street Journal* (March 23, 2004): D2.

Cohen, Hal. "The Baby Bias." *New York Times* (August 4, 2004): A4.

Cohen, Patricia. "Mothering and Its Cultural Discontents." *New York Times* (March 24, 2004): E7.

Electionline. "Heinz Kerry Retracts 'Real Job' Comment." *USA Today* (October 21, 2004): A4.

Herbert, Bob. "Living on Borrowed Money." *New York Times* (November 10, 2003): A21.

Hopkins, Jim. "More Moms, Fewer Pops." *USA Today* (October 20, 2003): B3.

Hymowitz, Carol. "Women Often Discover Their Business Talent after Kids Are Raised." *Wall Street Journal* (June 14, 2005): B1.

Krasnow, Iris. "It's Time to End the 'Mommy Wars.'" *Washington Post* (May 7, 1999): C5.

McGuire, Tim. "Women Can Find Meaning at Home as Well as at Work." *St. Louis Post-Dispatch* (March 8, 2004): C1.

Meltz, Barbara F. "Dads Are No Longer the 'Assistant Parent.'" *Boston Globe* (June 16, 2005): H1.

Shellenbarger, Sue. "Number of Au Pairs Increases Sharply as Rule Change Allows Longer Stays." *Wall Street Journal* (February 10, 2005): D1.

———. "The Night Shift: Schools, PTAs Create Ways to Involve Working Parents." *Wall Street Journal* (December 2, 2004): D1.

———. "The Sole Breadwinner's Lament: Having Mom at Home Isn't as Great as It Sounds." *Wall Street Journal* (October 16, 2003): D1.

———. "Women's Groups Give Peace a Chance in a War of At-Home and Working." *Wall Street Journal* (December 12, 2002): D1.

Stout, Hillary. "The New Family Portfolio Manager: Mom." *Wall Street Journal* (February 10, 2005): D1.

Uchitelle, Louis. "Job Track or 'Mommy Track'? Some Do Both, in Phases." *New York Times* (July 5, 2002): C1.

BIBLIOGRAPHY

Vuocolo, Jon. "Working Moms Catch Break in Court." *Wall Street Journal* (April 28, 2004): D3.

Zimmerman, Racheal. "The Carriage Trade: Stay-at-Home Moms Get Entrepreneurial." *Wall Street Journal* (October 21, 2004): 1.

WEB SITES

Belkin, Lisa. "The Opt Out Revolution." *New York Times*, October 26, 2003. http://www.nytimes.com/2003/10/26/magazine/26/WOMEN.html (accessed October 27, 2003).

Bender Consulting. "Company Information." http://www.bluesuitmom.org/company/ (accessed June 15, 2005).

Catalyst. "About Catalyst: Our Mission." http://www.catalystwomen.org/about/mission.shtml (accessed January 11, 2005).

Families and Work Institute. "Highlights of the 2002 National Study of the Changing Workforce." http://www.familiesandwork.org/about/index.html (accessed June 9, 2005).

Family and Home Network. "Frequently Asked Questions." http://www.familyandhome.org/org_overview.html (accessed January 11, 2005).

Flexible Resources. "20% of Women Seeking Flexibility Are Childless." http://www.flexibleresources.com/sub/news.html (accessed June 15, 2004).

———. "Many Women in Flexible Jobs are Family Breadwinners." http://www.flexibleresources.com/sub/news.html (accessed June 15, 2004).

The Motherhood Project. "About Us." http://www.watchoutforchildren.org/html/about_us.html (accessed January 11, 2005).

MOTHERS: Mothers Ought To Have Equal Rights. "About Us." http://www.mothersoughttohaveequalrights.org/about/ (accessed January 11, 2005).

Mothers and More. "About Us: What We Do." http://www.mothersandmore.org/AboutUs/about_us.shtml (accessed January 11, 2005).

National Association of Mothers' Centers. "About Us." http://www.motherscenter.org/about/index.html (accessed June 15, 2005).

9to5. "About Us." http://www.9to5.org/about/ (accessed January 11, 2005).

Paul, Pamela. "What Moms Want Now; Second-Guessing Your Choice about Whether to Work or Not? Join the Club: Our Groundbreaking Survey Reveals a Fascinating New Shift in What Mothers Today Are Really Yearning For." *Redbook,* March 2003. http://www.web7.infotrac.galegroup.com/itw/infomark/591/883/52465874w7/purl=rcl_GRGM... (accessed October 15, 2004).

Pletichen, Kim. "The Mommy Wars: The Case for a Ceasefire." http://www.mothersmovement.org/features/cease_fire/cease_fire_pl.htm (accessed January 21, 2005).

WorknMom. "About Us." http://www.worknmom.com/aboutus.html (accessed June 15, 2005).

OTHER

Dr. Phil. "Mom versus Mom" and "Mom versus Mom: Part II," episodes 216 and 346, first broadcast November 10, 2003, and September 3, 2004, respectively.

Market Probe International. "Prosumer Pulse2004: A Global Study—Anticipating Consumer Demand." Conducted for EuroRSCG Worldwide (February 2004): The Modern Day Father: U.S. and U.K., p. 5, and Education and Parenting, p. 3.

INDEX

INDEX

INDEX